Virtual Sociability: From Community to Communitas

VIRTUAL SOCIABILITY: FROM COMMUNITY TO COMMUNITAS

Selected papers from the Purdue
Online Interaction Theory Seminar

Volume 1

A ubibook guided by your mobile phone

SORIN ADAM MATEI

BRIAN C. BRITT

EDITORS

InterAcademic Press, 2011
http://ubimark.com

2011
InterAcademic is an Ideagora imprint
Published and printed in
the United States
http://ubimark.com & http://ideagora.us

Cover Illustration, Emrah Turudu, all rights reserved
http://www.istockphoto.com/stock-photo-1051394-wired-
business.php

This book can be purchased through Amazon.com at:

http://ubimark.com/in/link/90

ISBN: 978-1461003120
LCCN: 2011904536

Ideagora, LLC
PO BOX 40551
Indianapolis, IN
46240
United States of America
Email: media@ideagora.us
Web: http://ideagora.us

Table of Contents

Introduction

Sorin Adam Matei

http://ubimark.com/in/books/996/

Every day, across the Web, from Phnom Phen to Seattle, and from Bucharest to Johannesburg, thousands if not millions of groups of people who have never met each other in person exchange information, form organizations, help each other, start companies, trade jokes or insults, jostle for attention, or, turning to Clausewitz's famous quip which Al Qaeda illustrates so well, wage war by other means. These interactions take place in the comment spaces of online newspapers spanning a broad gamut, from the Cambodian *Phnom Phen Post* and the Romanian *Evenimentul Zilei* to the *South African Post* and *MSNBC*. They stretch from the blog of Lilick Auftakt, the premiere liberal voice of Romania, to the South African president Jacob Zuma's Facebook page or to that mother of all political gossip aggregators, the Huffington Post. They include, for good measure, the world famous GGMB (Gymnastics gossip message board), the IBS (irritable bowel syndrome) constellation of support fora, and—why not?—the Russian president's Twitter account:

@medvedevrussiae

To what degree can the human exchanges we observe in these spaces be called "sociability"? In other words, do the exchanges amount to any meaningful type of social organization? Are they more than the mere froth of collective emotion discharging its energy with a lot of noise but little consequence against the wave breakers

VIRTUAL SOCIABILITY

Sorin Adam Matei

 of social media? Do the social interactions that take place in virtual space—all those kind or not-so-kind words sent back and forth—suggest the same level of commitment, dedication, morality, passion, or even depravity that we see in everyday life? Or, more succinctly, is sociability online less "social," less "real" than what we see in everyday life? Are the groups that interact online of less consequence than those that gather offline? If not, is online sociability characterized by a set of attributes that puts it on a different (perhaps superior) level of human interactivity, as some luminaries of online media presaged some time ago (Hiltz & Turoff, 1978; Licklider & Taylor, 1968; Nelson, 1987; Rheingold, 2002)?

These questions were discussed, dissected, analyzed, interrogated, and put to rest one semester only to be revived the next by a group of extraordinary graduate students enrolled in the Online Interaction seminar which I have been teaching at Purdue University since 2003. The seminar syllabus summarizes the mission of the course in these terms:

"As more and more traditional institutions and groups move their transactions online, the need to understand the relevant advantages and disadvantages inherent in the new media has increased. The present course will discuss the social, organizational, and design implications of online social interaction. It will discuss traditional and newer social theory related to organizational and social interaction in the context of online groups. At the same time, the students will be exposed to the main theoretical and practical literature related to Web usability and

2

community design in an online context."
(http://matei.org/url/ointclass)

The present collection of papers reflects some of the most insightful seminar contributions that aimed to get at the theoretical underpinnings of online sociability. They reflect the individual interpretive frameworks that the members of the course found most inspiring or productive. As the readers will notice, the conversation is circumscribed by a number of themes, of which two are most important. The first one is related to the nature of online sociability. Are or could online groups be "community-like," bound by ties as strong as those of kith and kin? Or should they be qualified as a type of contractual, rational, self-interested "society" (Tönnies, 1964). Or, for that matter, should we propose a new interpretive framework? Should online communities seen as a type of "communitas"?

As the course instructor I proposed this last perspective as a "third way," which would leave behind the sterile discussion about the "reality" and "unreality" of online groups. Proposing communitas as a theoretical framework was, I believe, benefic. (Of course, only the reader can measure its effects by reading the chapters of this book). As defined by Turner, communitas is a type of social aggregation that is characterized by a transient, liminal state that mixes a variety of contradictory characteristics (temporary and permanent, close and distant, essential and fleeting), in which individuals come together as one, are transformed, and returned to society renewed, reinvigorated or even dramatically transformed.

VIRTUAL SOCIABILITY

Sorin Adam Matei

 Applying communitas to understanding social interactions online also involved a transformative theoretical enterprise of our own. The most stimulating was probably the proposition that communitas, a concept that was circumscribed to very specific ritualized, *hic et nunc* interactions (e.g., a Christian Mass or a Nuer rite of passage), might also be employed as a master term for explaining the ethos of interaction in online environments. In effect, I proposed communitas as a broad "cultural pattern," as a set of assumptions super-determined by a group of values. Communitas, at least as it is employed here, is not a concept that entirely overlaps Tönnies' "society" or "community" since it does not share all their attributes, especially the supposed existence of a "collective will" of some sort. Communitas is a term that suggests an altogether new and contradictory type of sociability, which implies a will to be together, but also the desire to individualize and distance oneself from others. In this respect I followed some of the concepts I proposed in my paper "From counterculture to cyberculture," especially the idea that virtual sociability, at least as an ideal, is a late-modern form of social aggregation that is profoundly ambiguous (Matei, 2005). I believe that this perspective allows us to better deal with a number of intractable problems, such as the simultaneous fleetingness and fluidity of online groups and their ability to muster energies and commitments at times superior to those we could encounter in real life.

The second major theme of debate in our seminar that is reflected in the chapters of this book is the role played by conflict in online social interaction. One of the most intriguing conclusions of our conversations was

4

Introduction

http://ubimark.com/in/books/996/

that conflict in online groups cannot and should not be explained away as a side effect or as an exception to the rule, but instead should be treated as a defining element of online interaction. Conflict (verbal, emotional, ideological,  etc.) is a *sui generis* binding element, a type of social glue. Through conflict, individuals participating in online interaction define the boundaries of their groups and of their own identities. They create and recreate their identities, and most importantly, they maintain their social environs in the fluid state necessary for maintaining "communitas." Confrontation is ritualized at times and turned into an initiation wherein those capable of withstanding ridicule or who, better yet, come out on top after an argument, become members of the inner sanctum of the "chosen" interaction leaders.

This insight emerged through parallel reading of Howard Rheingold's (2000) *Virtual Community* and John Seabrook's (1997) *Deeper*, two seminal but very different early explorations of one of the earliest and most articulated spaces for debate and social interaction online, the much vaunted Well "virtual community." We found the Well particularly germane for our discussion, first because of its social makeup (it was, for a long time, the place to be if you wanted to keep in touch with the Grateful Dead community), but also because its ideology of in-your-face, "you own your words" libertarianism and unfettered freedom of expression reflected the countercultural values of its creator, the editor of the Whole Earth Catalogue, Steward Brand.

Reading the two books in parallel and exploring the social style of the Well, we realized that conflict, as Rheingold, one of the members of the Well, tells

VIRTUAL SOCIABILITY

Sorin Adam Matei

 Seabrook, a "newbie" trying to break into the inner sanctum of the Well cognoscenti, is "an initiation ritual. Stick around and help us dump on the next guy. ;-)" (Seabrook, 1997, p. 177). This ritualized application of conflict seems to be validated by the manner in which succeeding waves of more or less online "social" media thrived on creating and maintaining controversies. Making it in the social media world often involves creating or stirring up controversy, as was the case for Matt Drudge's meteoric career. Blogs and blogging inspired a new type of political militancy and collaboration, illustrated by the flash mobs of writers who ruined Trent Lott's (Scott, 2004) and Dan Rather's (Messner & Distaso, 2008; Pein, 2005) careers. Recent research highlights that controversy similarly plays an important role in shaping the environment in which Wikipedia articles are edited (Kittur, Lee, & Kraut, 2009; Kittur, Suh, Pendleton, & Chi, 2007; Matei & Dobrescu, 2011).

However, the papers reunited in this book are not completely circumscribed to these topics. Social identity, social negotiation of meaning and the individualistic propensities of online communities are also debated, and intriguing answers are provided by the contributors. I leave to the readers the pleasure of discovering them.

As a final note about the paper selection and about the broader meaning of this initiative, I should add that over the years several cohorts of students have taken the Online Interaction seminar, totaling more than 50 individuals. Of these contributions, we have selected those that were the best articulated, which aimed not only to discuss known issues, but also to propose innovative perspectives. In this respect, this collection

6

Introduction

http://ubimark.com/in/books/996/

of papers aims to continue a tradition that has been unfortunately discontinued in American social scientific graduate education.  Many of the social science advanced seminars used to publish their best papers as a way not only to encourage their students to excel, but also to disseminate knowledge that would otherwise be lost. Our project aims to rekindle this tradition, enhancing it with all that social media can offer us to disseminate the good news about the exciting research conducted at Purdue University.

References

Hiltz, S. R., & Turoff, M. (1978). The Network Nation: Human Communication via Computer. New York, NY: Addison-Wesley.

Kittur, A., Lee, B., & Kraut, R. E. (2009). Coordination in collective intelligence: The role of team structure and task interdependence. In CHI 2009: Proceedings of the ACM Conference on Human-factors in Computing Systems (pp. 1495-1504). New York: ACM Press.

Kittur, A., Suh, B., Pendleton, B. A., Chi., E. (2007). He says, she says: Conflict and coordination in Wikipedia. In CHI 2007: Proceedings of the ACM Conference on Human-factors in Computing Systems (pp. 453-462). New York: ACM Press.

Licklider, J. C. R., & Taylor, R. W. (1968). The computer as a communication device. Science and Technology, 76, 21-31.

Matei, S. A. (2005). From counterculture to cyberculture: Virtual community discourse and the dilemma of modernity. Journal of Computer Mediated Communication, 10(3). Retrieved from http://jcmc.indiana.edu/vol10/issue3/matei.html

VIRTUAL SOCIABILITY

Sorin Adam Matei

 Matei, S. A., & Dobrescu, C. (2011). Wikipedia's "Neutral Point of View": Settling conflict through ambiguity. The Information Society, 27(1), 40-51.

Messner, M., & DiStaso, M. W. (2008). The source cycle: How traditional media and weblogs use each other as sources. Journalism Studies, 9(3), 447-463.

Nelson, T. H. (1987). Computer lib. Dream machines (Rev.). Redmond, Wash.: Tempus Books of Microsoft Press.

Pein, C. (2005). Blog-Gate: Yes, CBS screwed up badly in 'Memogate' but so did those who covered the affair. Columbia Journalism Review, 43(5), 30-35.

Rheingold, H. (2000). The virtual community: homesteading on the electronic frontier (2nd ed.). Cambridge, MA: MIT Press.

Rheingold , H. (2002). Smart mobs: The next social revolution. Cambridge, MA: Perseus.

Seabrook, J. (1997). Deeper. New York, NY: Simon & Schuster.

Scott, E. (2004). 'Big Media' Meets the 'Blogger': Coverage of Trent Lott's Remarks at Strom Thurmond's Birthday Party. Kennedy School of Government Case Program. Retrieved from http://www.ksg.harvard.edu/presspol/Research_Publications/Case_Studies/17 31_0.pdf

Tönnies, F. (1964). Gemeinschaft und Gesellschaft. Community and Society. New York: Harper and Row.

The book is dead! Long live the ubibook!

Sorin Adam Matei

http://ubimark.com/in/books/641/

So, what is a *ubibook*? And how could a book be *guided* by your mobile phone? It's quite simple. The book links the printed text to a discussion space that resides on the Internet. Your mobile device is a magnifying glass that can make Internet information visible while you read the book. This magic is performed with the help of a little piece of technology, called a 2-D code.

This book is enhanced with all the wonderful things brought about by the latest Web technologies: online social interaction, interactive discussions, and on-demand video. What you are holding in your hands is a springboard. The arguments presented on paper are just a starting point. With the help of the Internet and of a mobile phone you will be able to interact with the authors of the book and with other readers. You can also listen to brief video messages posted by the authors.

The book is, however, more than a one-way information pipeline. You are invited to join and participate in the online community that is connected to the book. The book is a social interface. Through it, you will interact not only with computers but also with real people who share your interest for online interaction and facilitation theories and applications. The book will connect you with a group of scholars and graduate students who work together through the Internet to enhance and improve the "Virtual Sociability" experience. This group congregates in cyberspace, using

Sorin Adam Matei

 mobile phones or the Web-based version of the book, hosted at ubimark.com.

As you read along, you are invited to express your thoughts with your fellow readers. These contributions will be incorporated in future editions of the printed book as footnotes and hyperlinks. The book will change with the needs, desires, and ideas of the community of its readers.

How do you do it?

All this might sound like a tall tale. How can you digitally connect people through a book made of dead trees? And how can we incorporate future comments in a book that has already been published? It's actually quite simple. Here is the trick:

We start by connecting plain paper pages to the Internet through 2-D codes. These are the mysterious stamp-sized graphics on the cover of the book, the marker at the top of this page, or those found in the header of each page starting with chapter 1. The most concise way to explain their role in this project is: "printed hyperlinks." They are the younger siblings of the barcodes used by grocery stores to read product prices. Like these, 2-D codes contain information, which is stored in the random-looking pixels that pepper them. In this book, however, the markers say nothing about the price of the book. Instead, they contain an Internet address. When scanned, they bring up an Internet page, file, or video clip.

The beauty of 2-D codes is that you do not need specialized scanners to read them. 2-D codes can be interpreted by most camera-enabled cell phones that also support a 2-D code application, such as i-nigma

The book is dead! Long live the ubibook!

http://ubimark.com/in/books/641/

(http://i-nigma.mobi), our preferred code reader. A 2-D code application is a small program that enables your phone to interpret the markers and retrieve content from the Internet. If you have an iPhone, you know what I am talking  about: an app. If you have a Windows Mobile or other type of phone, the app is very similar to your applications for opening files or playing music. Installing it is as simple as installing a new mp3 player. As already mentioned, our preferred scanning application is that provided by i-nigma. In what follows I will provide you with the broader overview of what this technology does and how it can be used.

How does it work?

This is how 2-D codes work. If your phone has a camera, can connect to the Internet, and has an appropriate code reader/scanner installed, your cell phone will serve as a code scanner and media player. In most cases, and especially when using i-nigma, all you have to do is start your 2-D code scanning application and point the phone to the code. The phone will recognize the code for what it is (hyperlink or text message) and will load the appropriate application. If it is a hyperlink, it will bring up a Web browser. If the file at the end of the hyperlink carries audio or video information, an appropriate player will be fired up. The file will start playing without your further intervention. The codes in the chapter headers will always take you to the Web versions of the text, where comments can be added or read on your mobile phone.

What if your phone cannot use the code reader? If you have an Internet connection, you can enter the URLs provided under or above each code in any Internet-

Sorin Adam Matei

 ready phone Web browser. Or, of course, you can use your computer. To start, visit the online version of the book at

http://ubimark.com/in/books/590

Enjoy!

Why?

At the end of this introduction, some of you might wonder, "If they offer an online version of the book, why should I bother with the effort and expense involved in buying the book? Why should I mess around with these 2-D codes and mobile phone applications, and so on? Why not, for example, read the book directly in the iPhone browser or on my computer? Aren't we going to get rid of paper-based media soon, anyway?" My brief answer is: No! Here is why.

I believe that until computer screens match pixel by pixel and lumen by lumen the level of resolution, contrast or the natural luminosity of the light reflected by paper, electronic screens will be useful only for short documents. In my honest opinion, when it comes to reading scholarly book-long narratives, good old paper pages do a better job. They are better at keeping us focused. The light reflected by them feels more natural. The finer edges of printed letters provide better visual anchors. In addition, the wavelength of the light that hits our retina is precisely that intended by God, Shiva, Manitou, or Mother Nature for our eyes. Should I add that books are more portable, more reliable, and sturdier than a computer screen? Or that they are almost waterproof and/or easily replaceable? Their use requires less cognitive effort. Books are easier to flip

The book is dead! Long live the ubibook!

http://ubimark.com/in/books/641/

through, and they offer a more directly intuitive sense for which part of the book is what part of the story. They do not crash. They do not need to be plugged in. Books are considerably lighter. And by the way, reading a book  does not require a chair or a desk. An armchair or a plushy carpet is often enough.

But what about e-ink technologies, such as those used by Amazon's Kindle, an example of which you can find at http://ubimark.com/in/link/80? These tablet devices are small, easy to use and have no flicker. They use reflected light, just like paper, and can be read lying on the floor, too.

They are a worthy opponent, but there are two major drawbacks, at least in their current incarnation. First, their screen contrast is not that great. The white of their background is never bright white. It oscillates between various shades of gray. Neither are the letters pitch-dark. They are at most a dark gray. Basically, their screens offer a gray on gray reading experience.

Furthermore, few of the current reading tablets support full Internet connectivity. They have no hyperlinks or permanent connections to the Internet. They cannot play video files or display maps, and the pictures they display are reminiscent of the era of dot matrix printers and text art. Thus, a book printed on great paper that can connect to a cell phone and from here further on to the Internet, makes more sense.

Don't get me wrong, though. I am no Luddite, nor too wrapped in our little project not to see that much progress will be made in the future in terms of displays and connectivity. I cannot wait for the time when displays will be just as bright, feel as natural to the touch or eye, or be as bendable as paper is today. I am

Sorin Adam Matei

 itching to get a reading tablet on which pictures will look just as glamorous as they look in a magazine. Some say, the future is already here and its name is Apple iPad. Since I am writing this right after Apple announced the device, but before seeing an iPad in person, Zhou Enlai's famous quip about the French Revolution is the best I can think of. Once, Mao's closest comrade and architect of the US-China rapprochement was asked for his assessment of the 1789 event. He answered, "It's too soon to tell!"

In the meantime, join our experiment.

How will the book incorporate your contributions?

You can become a contributor simply by commenting on the chapters. When you scan 2-D codes found in the header of each chapter, a Web page with links to comment boxes is served to your mobile phone. You can share your thoughts with us immediately. If you want to type a longer message, go to the site and post another message.

If you decide to help us by joining the commenter and contributor community at http://ubimark.com, your work will be included in the future versions of the book, which we hope to release every few months. We use the Amazon.com print-on-demand system, which means that each book is individually printed when ordered. We periodically update the master file of the book, in which we include any worthy link, comment, or other type of content contributed by the readers. The information that is to be included in future versions of the book is sorted, edited, and vetted by the graduate students at Purdue University enrolled in the Online Interaction course. We also are planning to streamline the editing

The book is dead! Long live the ubibook!

http://ubimark.com/in/books/641/

and publishing system. Individual comments and additions will be immediately and selectively added to the master file. Each contributor can publish a custom version of the book, which incorporates his or her own  comments and additions right after adding them. The technology is already available and has been used in a number of WordPress plugins. All we need to do is to devise some API magic.

Acknowledgments

This project would have not been possible without the open-software, free-content revolution. Most of the software used in this book is open source and/or free. A heartfelt thank-you goes out to all those who made this possible at Purdue University: Candiss Vibbert, Beverly Sypher, Ryan Scott, Jim Krogmeier, Howard Sypher, Rebecca Ivic, Jeannine Phipps, Nicholas Rogers, and the several generations of students that have fueled the debates in the basement of Beering Hall, where our seminar usually meets.

Finally, my thanks, hugs, and gratitude go to my wife and my kids, who are still wondering what I am mumbling about while playing with my iPhone.

Sorin Adam Matei
Associate Professor
Purdue University
2011

User Guide

Sorin Adam Matei

http://ubimark.com/in/books/1061/

We have looked long and hard for the best code reader out there and have decided upon **I-NIGMA**. It is widely available, installs without a flaw, and requires minimal user intervention. The i-nigma team, which to my knowledge toils away at this product in the faraway Israel (Shalom, friends!), has ported the 2d code reader to a large number of phones, so I hope yours will be among those supported. If not, you can try a different code reader, such as that provided by kaywa at http://kaywa.net. I have provided at the end of this chapter a longer list of resources.

Requirements
To scan and use 2d codes, your mobile phone should have:
- A camera
- A connection to the Internet (i.e., a "data plan")
- A Web browser
- A media player

If you have none of these tools, you can still communicate with the reader community of "Around the world in 80 Days" via text messages. Simply text "join 80d" to 8762 (in the U.S.). Regular texting charges will apply. We get nothing (nada, zero, zilch) from the carriers, so don't blame us if the phone bill gets too high from your addiction.

In addition, using our resources is free, but sending and receiving data, in the form of audio or video files, might cost you a penny or more if your provider charges by the volume of your traffic. Make sure you monitor your data traffic and, if needed, switch to an unlimited data plan. Again, we make no money from the data transfer, so do not blame us if the phone bill gets too high.

Drum roll! Here is how you install your app:

iPhones

Press the App Store button. Search for "i-nigma" (use the dash and make sure you type an "i" at the beginning). Load the free version of the i-nigma reader. When done, tap the icon. Point the camera at one of the markers. See what happens. If you do not like i-nigma, you can also try neoreader, quickmark, scanlife or any other reader that suits your fancy. To find alternative readers, type "2d code" or "qr code" in the App Store search box.

Windows Mobile/Pocket PC Phones

If your phone is a smartphone running on a Windows-based operating system, open up your Web browser. In most cases, that would be Internet Explorer. Type http://i-nigma.mobi in the address bar. Your phone will immediately be recognized, and you will be provided a link and information for downloading the application.

If the trick does not work, your OS might be very, very, very old. How about you indulge yourself by getting a new phone?

VIRTUAL SOCIABILITY

Sorin Adam Matei

Blackberry Phones

Try the same trick as above. The phone should be automatically recognized. If this does not work, again, get a new phone, or an iPhone, or try any of the other links listed for "all other phones" below.

Android

Take your Android in your hand. Go to Android Market. Search for "barcode scanner." Choose i-nigma or another reader of your own choice. Go.

All Other Phones

1. Go to http://i-nigma.mobi
   If your phone is compatible, you will get a link and instructions how to download the application.
2. If this does not work with your phone, go to http://getscanlife.com
3. If this does not work either, then try http://reader.kaywa.com
4. If this does not work, then next visit http://get.neoreader.com
5. If none of the above options work, try this link: http://ubimark.com/in/link/77

Front Porches and Public Spaces: Planned Communities Online

Susan Huelsing Sarapin

http://ubimark.com/in/books/577/

Abstract

This article presents and critically assesses the person-centered, non-technical mechanisms by which organic Internet communities are initiated and sustained, the principles and practices that form the foundation for these communities, and the methods used to maintain them and by which their viability can be evaluated. It first takes a look at the history of communities on the Web by tracing the origin of purposive community construction online to the WELL, The Whole Earth 'Lectronic Link, formed as a commercial enterprise in 1985. It then addresses the characteristics, scale, and affordances of an earthly prototype, the first American planned community called Seaside in Florida. Finally, there is a discussion about the meaning of a "sense of community," its components of membership, influence, fulfillment of needs, and shared emotional connection, and how these inform the core mechanisms and principles for building and maintaining virtual community.

Introduction

Where else today but in the cost-effective frontier of cyberspace can the average person construct a community?[1] With widespread availability of open-source (free) software applications for just about any use imaginable, a person with minimal computer literacy, a few hours, and $20–30 a month to spare can establish  the functional framework for an online community. Of course, anyone who has ever published a site on the Internet is well aware of the implausibility of the nineties' ubiquitous catchphrase from the movie Field of Dreams, "If you build it, they will come" (Gordon, Gordon, & Robinson, 1989). That bromide could have had only a very small window of opportunity, if any at all, within which to be considered true in regard to online communities, and that window would have been in the early 1990s.

Cyberspace is chock-full of communities of every stripe, from social networks to professional information exchanges. If a site developed with community as a goal has not been well-conceived at the outset, adeptly moderated and maintained, and frequently evaluated to determine if refinements are needed, the "community" may attract dozens or hundreds of users for a time or two, but it will never achieve the critical mass necessary for survival. This paper will present and critically assess

---

[1] There is no scientific consensus on the definition of "community." For the sake of simplicity, this paper uses the Random House definition as follows:

[A] social, religious, occupational, or other group sharing common characteristics or interests and perceived or perceiving itself as distinct in some respect from the larger society within which it exists (usually prec. by the): the business community; the community of scholars (Random House Unabridged Dictionary, 2006)

Susan Huelsing Sarapin

 the person-centered, non-technical mechanisms by which Internet communities are initiated and sustained, the principles and practices that form the foundation for these communities, and the methods used to maintain them and by which their viability can be evaluated. In order to put these tenets of successful online community building into perspective, we will first look at the history of communities on the Web, and point to when and how social scientists began to involve themselves in the study of these organic entities.

A Brief History of Online Communities

The subject of online community is relatively new in academic literature because experimentation itself in the building of community into Internet "spaces" is only about 20 years old. Rheingold was one of the first people to write about the experience by describing what is commonly recognized as the grand, social adventure in online community building called the WELL, The Whole Earth 'Lectronic Link, which was founded in 1985 as a commercial enterprise (Figallo, 1993). Although the WELL was not initially launched with community per se in mind, but rather as a Web-based affordance for public conversation in the form of a computer conferencing system, it evolved into what Rheingold later coined as a "virtual community" (Rheingold, 1993). Rheingold defines "virtual communities" as "[S]ocial aggregations that emerge from the Net when enough people carry on those public discussions long enough, with sufficient human feeling, to form webs of personal relationships in cyberspace" (Rheingold, 1993, p. xx).

Cliff Figallo, another early netizen, writes about the WELL in terms of its community characteristics when he calls it a "small town on the Internet highway system" (Figallo, 1993). By way of explaining its longevity, Figallo  (1993) states that it "has survived primarily through the online personal interaction of its subscribers and staff rather than through successful business strategy developed by its owners and managers." Clearly, he is asserting that although the WELL wasn't planned as a community, its ultimate transformation into one was due to the sociability of its participants.

The WELL spawned numerous other computer-mediated, social aggregations on the Internet, and as computer technology began to make advances in hardware and software applications, public gathering places in cyberspace became more efficient, user friendly, affordable, and ubiquitous. Much has been written about the WELL as the prototype for today's virtual communities, but the theories behind the planned shaping of online social and networking behavior leading to community constitute a new area of communication research. Since as recently as 2000, just six years ago, the phenomenon of online sociability engineering has been a topic of serious research when a few social scientists began to look at it as an offshoot of real-world community building. Extrapolating from human behavior theories borrowed from the fields of sociology and social psychology, communication specialists have developed their own theories of and principles for building, maintaining, and evaluating online communities (Preece, 2000, p. 148). To better understand the dynamics and effects of interaction in cyberspace, it is instructive to review some of the

Susan Huelsing Sarapin

 sociological theories underlying human group interaction in planned, brick-and-mortar communities.

Real-World Planned Community

In the actual non-digital, physical realm, developers collaborate with city planners and forward-thinking architects to build residential neighborhoods planned to evolve into self-contained, self-governing, mixed-use pseudo-towns made up of a post office, entertainment venues, a "town" hall, and other public spaces. The channels of sociability are built into the physical framework of the community with human-scaled living as a guiding principle. The Village Tannin (http://www.villagetannin.com/) in Orange Beach, Alabama is just such a community that was built to simulate the town of Seaside (http://www.seasidefl.com/) on the gulf-coast panhandle of Florida, considered by most to be the granddaddy of this genre. These two "villages" are examples of what are called "planned communities." They represent developments arising from the New Urbanism philosophy, which emerged in the late 1980s and early 1990s, and are characterized by walkable neighborhoods, open spaces, architectural covenants and environmental aesthetics, modified street grids, greater facility for pedestrian traffic, a central square, a school within walking distance from all homes, narrow streets, and front porches (Congress for the New Urbanism, 2006).

Although this movement came out of a desire to find an alternative to urban sprawl and its objectionable sequelae by emphasizing physical layout, its planned communities market themselves as places in which their residents can enjoy a "sense of community." The

Village Tannin puts it this way on its
Web site: "Getting to know your
neighbors as a natural part of daily
living lessens the sense of isolation so
often found in today's large, modern
subdivisions and gives residents a
greater sense of community and security" (The Village
Tannin, 2006).

In providing a description of what the sense of
community construct would include, Plas and Lewis
(1996) quote Sarason (1974, p. 157): "the perception of
similarity to others, an acknowledged interdependence
by giving to or doing for others what one expects from
them, the feeling that one is part of a larger dependable
and stable structure" (Plas & Lewis, 1996, p. 1). Unger
and Wandersman (1985) attribute three characteristics
to the construct when they suggest "the social
component, including emotional and instrumental
support and social networks; the cognitive component,
including cognitive mapping of the physical
environment and symbolic communication; and the
affective component, or the emotional attachment
individuals have to persons living around them" (Plas &
Lewis, p. 1).

The most frequently cited definition of "sense of
community" as it relates to geographically oriented
communities is that of McMillan and Chavis (1986).
Their research has demonstrated that the four major
elements of the construct are as follows:

1. membership, whose five traits are boundaries,
emotional safety, a sense of belonging and
identification, personal investment, and a common
symbol system

2. influence, a feeling that what one does and says
matters or makes a difference

Susan Huelsing Sarapin

3. fulfillment of needs, shared values, membership status and what benefits come from it, perceived similarity to others, and an economy of social trade
4. shared emotional connection

As we will soon see, these four components are strikingly similar to those posited by several communication specialists who have written extensively on the topic of Web-based community and communities of practice.

Shepherding Community Ideals on the Internet

One cannot even begin to think about launching a site intended for community until thoroughly understanding the elements necessary for community to happen. Consequently, we must do our due diligence by defining what community is. As Preece (2000) articulately cautions Internet developers,

> [C]ommunities are neither designed nor do they just emerge. How software is designed affects community development just as the architecture of a house affects those who live in it. How people interact in a community shapes its long-term evolution. And though people's behavior cannot be controlled, it can be influenced (p. 6).

Preece then identifies the two concepts she feels not only lie at the heart of the process of developing online communities but also provide the framework for evaluating them, sociability and usability (pp. 7–8). This discussion focuses on the sociability factor, the mechanisms by which large-scale interpersonal interaction is fostered in the enthusiastically anticipated evolution of community in cyberspace.

Consistent with but not identical to the definition proposed by McMillan and Chavis (1986), Preece (2000), a proponent of operationalizing the theories of sociologists and psychologists, proffers her own considered assumptions about the meaning of "community" as it applies to online constructs. She identifies the four primary criteria for deeming an online aggregation of people a community as (a) people socially interacting with each other in order to satisfy their own needs or perform specific roles; (b) a shared purpose that provides a reason for the community's existence; (c) policies exemplified by rules, rituals, and protocols that guide people's behavior; and (d) computer systems that support and facilitate sociability and a sense of togetherness (p. 10).

The fourth item in her list is more closely related to the technical or usability facet of the entire process as she typifies it, but it could easily be modified into a more sociability-related term by calling this the human moderator/mediator criterion. The computer systems and software are more like the houses, streets, and public buildings so necessary for the habitation of a neighborhood by an aggregation of people. They provide the infrastructure or "place" and "space" for people to gather, and it makes sociability possible, but it does not necessarily ensure a sense of community.

Wenger, McDermott, and Snyder (2002) provide a succinct definition of "community of practice," and then explicate each of its components in much greater detail. They say that it is "a group of people who interact, learn together, build relationships, and in the process develop a sense of belonging and mutual commitment" (p. 34). Their definition includes the concept of learning

Susan Huelsing Sarapin

together, which is essential in a group that comes together specifically to share knowledge. The sharing of knowledge, per se, is not necessarily the reason for other groups of people to form communities, but as we see in so many proposed definitions of "community," shared purpose underlying social interaction is.

Powazek (2002), a writer, Web designer, and community consultant, concisely expresses his definition of online communities in only 23 words: "Web communities happen when users are given tools to use their voice in a public and immediate way, forming intimate relationships over time" (p. xxii). Just as Preece and Wenger et al. do, Powazek expounds upon his definitional elements by laying out the principles of successful community building, maintenance, and evaluation derived from them. And now that we have a firm understanding of what community is, we can investigate the principles for developing and sustaining one online.

Core Mechanisms and Principles for Building Community on the Web

Due to the nature of human behavior, these guidelines sometimes overlap, and can simultaneously contribute to the effectiveness of two or more foundational components of the community.

Membership. One of the overarching themes that emerges from most definitions of successful real-world and online communities is that of membership or the sense of belonging to something larger than oneself. Many considerations go into the development of belongingness.

http://ubimark.com/in/books/577/

Principle 1: The community must be geared toward a pre-determined, identifiable audience. Certainly, one of the first issues to be given attention in order to facilitate the sense of belonging is that of identifying the  audience, the participants who will be targeted to engage in the site's interactions and whose contributions will dictate the community's purpose and help mold its personality. A developer must determine the demographics of the intended audience, what its initial unifying goal will be, the relevant topic of discussion that will constitute its theme, its members' age range, cultural and intellectual make-up, gender distribution, and more. A catchy, clever, short, representative name should be carefully selected to most aptly identify the group and its purpose. Whether the developer likes it or not, the audience members will be the movers and shakers and molders of every characteristic of the community if one evolves.

Principle 2: The community Web site must be seeded with audience-relevant, engaging content that models the type of content expected of its participants. Another aspect that has a large impact on the membership characteristic of a community is its content. A site meant to serve a specific audience must be seeded with high-quality, relevant content before even the first person completes a membership form. The content is determined by the audience's goals and purpose, and serves as the fulcrum of textual communication, models the quality and type of verbal interaction, and reflects the shared interests of the group so anyone coming to the site knows the community's identity and voice right away. It is also through content that a common language, system of symbols, and acceptance of cultural

Susan Huelsing Sarapin

 differences emerge. Content also spills over into the area of participants satisfying their own needs by deriving pleasure and gaining information through the contributions of the other members and moderators.

Principle 3: Draw boundaries around the community and establish barriers to entry. The setting of boundaries is another facet of belongingness and identity. Part of making membership in a community meaningful is making it difficult for everyone to belong to it. If one must expend a certain amount of energy to join and truly become a part of the community, then he/she will have made an investment in something that a group is trying to build (Powazek, pp. 168–169). If anyone and everyone can join without any effort, then there is no cachet associated with membership and the identity of the group becomes diluted and nebulous. Exclusion is not necessarily a bad thing, and does not detract from the democracy within the community.

Intimate Relationships over Time. Wenger et al. (2002) agree with Preece regarding the impossibility of dictating interactive dynamism (p. 50). Acknowledging that communities are organic in nature, they state: "The goal of community design is to bring out the community's own internal direction, character, and energy" (p. 51). Preece (2000) describes the sociological perspective as indicating that perhaps the strength and kind of relationships among its residents are the most promising criteria for defining community (p. 15). Although these interpersonal relationships cannot be contrived, social interaction can be facilitated.

Principle 4: Enable participants to coordinate, cooperate, and collaborate with one another by setting up features that promote emotion-charged interaction and foster the acquisition of social capital. Preece (2000) purports that community norms of reciprocity, social trust and safety, and amplified status facilitate the resolution of social problems in online communities and  promote stronger ties between members. She continues: "Opportunism is reduced and opportunity for collaboration enhanced. 'I' centeredness tends to be converted into 'we' centeredness" (p. 24).

A part of this social capital is the members' belief that their ideas, points of view, and personalities will be valued simply in their individual contributions to the make-up of the whole. The members must feel safe and trusting that cultural, religious, philosophical, and gender differences will be appreciated as beautiful pieces stitched into the fabric of the patchwork quilt known as their community.

Principle 5: Provide and encourage an environment of hospitality, sharing, honesty, empathy and growth for exchanges between two people and between larger groups of people. This is what the adherents of the New Urbanism provide with their front porches and compact design with the pedestrian in mind. While a resident is walking along a sidewalk or narrow, tree-lined street, he/she comes into fairly close contact with other residents sitting on their porches. Spontaneous conversation has an opportunity to happen. Perhaps in the course of the pleasantries, the pedestrian is asked onto the porch for a glass of iced tea or lemonade. An acquaintanceship develops, and if the people involved find enough similarity of interests, the new relationship proves to be but a prelude to real friendship.

The concept of trust and security overlaps into this area as well. An online community must be a pleasant

Susan Huelsing Sarapin

 place to spend one's time. The moderators, hosts, and others in leadership must be gentle in their enforcement of policies and in their mediation of squabbles or other social dilemmas. In addition, those who have planned and continue to build and maintain the community must allow for the various types of communication within the community. For one thing, two people should be able to find a private place if need be, e.g., a chat room or a form of instant messaging, in which they can carry on a synchronous conversation out of view of the entire community.

Members should also be afforded venues for partially contemporaneous conversation such as what blog formats offer. These allow the "speakers" to review previous messages, reflect upon them, revise their own, and respond to others' postings. The qualities of review, reflection, and revision allow the conversation participants to find common ground with one another in a sharing environment. The theory of common ground "can be used as a framework for determining how two people or a small group validate that they understand each other" (Preece, 2000, pp. 156).

Fulfillment of Needs. It must be understood by the community developers and leaders that people will become members at first because of their personal expectations of what the other members will be able to provide them. Each will come to the site with a list of needs to be accommodated, most often without even a conscious realization of the list. According to one relatively recent appraisal of why people "hang out" in virtual communities, "Humans have a need to belong and be affiliated with others ...because groups provide individuals with a source of information and help in achieving goals" (Ridings & Gefen, 2004, p. xx, citing Watson & Johnson, 1972).

Ridings and Gefen (2004) also comment on the importance of friendship in online communities as a need that requires fulfillment for some. Friendships in virtual communities can provide additional benefits beyond that of information exchange and social support. The feeling of being together and being a member of a group of friends comes with the notions of being part of a group, spending time together, companionship, socializing, and networking. Friendship in this context is about the value of being together, unlike social support that deals with seeking emotional help or helping others.

Some Web surfers will come across an attractive site, read the home page, and instantly become engaged by its content. Some will get involved only with reading the site's blog entries because the subject matter is personally relevant. Another group will become actively involved in contributing content in the form of sharing personal and/or professional commentary regarding the topic of conversation because they perceive the community as vibrant and alive. And still others will share personal anecdotes, and receive in turn commiseration, validation, sympathy, empathy, appreciation, kudos, and more. Now these are just a few examples of why some online users remain at a site for a specified period of time.

Principle 6: Anticipate the need for the community to develop a history of its existence and textual interactions. If the participants never do, or cease to, get what they expected from the other community members, they will leave the community and go

Susan Huelsing Sarapin

 elsewhere to begin their search anew. One day, some of these transient members may come back to see if the community has evolved in any significant way that would bode well for a better "fit" this time within the group. Perhaps the intellectual level of the conversation has risen to meet the need for a more articulate level of discourse or a higher quality and reliability of shared information. Or maybe on the revisit, the user discovers a greater use of empathy or emotion in the messages...a more obvious camaraderie, good will, rapport, commonality, or familiarity. If the community seems to be different after a period of time, it has successfully adapted to the needs of the members who have guided the evolution. If it remains the substantially the same, but still maintains the same or greater number of members, than it can still be said that it has successfully attended to its members needs and possibly has added or enhanced features that the community demanded.

One way in which a newcomer to a community can evaluate how well the leadership has cared for its residents' needs is through a perusal of the community's archives, its history, so to speak. The history also serves to illustrate the community's identity and identify those participants who have remained members since the community's inception. So now that we have seen some of the more vital attributes necessary for building community online, we should take a look at some major aspects of sustaining a community.

http://ubimark.com/in/books/577/

Core Principles for Maintaining Community on the Web

Today, there are hundreds of thousands of Internet communities with more coming online every day, but their high failure rate points to either poor preparation and conceptualization before launching the site or poor management while the community is gaining traction and critical mass. In one research report on attempts to motivate online community members to contribute to the conversation, the authors explained that "in open-source development communities, 4% of members account for 50% of answers on a user-to-user help site" (Ling et al., 2005, p. xx; see also Lakhani & Hippel, 2003).

Principle 7: Find ways to make community contributors feel unique and that their contributions make a difference by fostering group ownership and a shared emotional connection. People are more likely to contribute to the community conversation when they feel unique or special (Ling et al., 2005, p. xx) Preece (2000) suggests encouraging community participants to verbally recognize the postings of others within the communication venue, acknowledge them in their responses, and reciprocate when one can. She also recommends that posters occasionally refer to the benefits they derive from membership in the community because it reinforces group commitment (p. 294).

Principle 8: Establish policies and rules of conduct using language and tone that indicates that the rules have been written to engender self-governance and a sense of personal ownership by the community members themselves. All virtual communities need rules, policies, and protocols for their survivability. This

35

Susan Huelsing Sarapin

 is actually a function of the development team before the site is launched, but at that time, the policies should be minimal and fundamentally nonrestrictive, and most important, communicated clearly and visibly (Powazek, p. 99). The role of good cop becomes a truly vital responsibility of the host or moderator once the group begins to see itself as a community. The policies are, and should be, fluid. They will be in a state of flux until the community has established itself as a viable and dynamic organism. The way the members want the behavior to be on their site will require modifications in order to model appropriate expression and action.

For example, if a person engages in an ad hominem attack (a.k.a. flaming) on another member because he doesn't respect the other person's opinions, the others in the group may feel that this is totally inappropriate behavior in their community. In order to maintain a civil and respectful tone of discussion, they would appeal to the moderator to create or enforce a rule against such attacks. Usually, a warning is enough to put an end to the bad behavior. If the warning fails to discourage the behavior, then the offending member is apt to lose his privilege of membership for a specified period of time.

Rules enforcing is but one responsibility of the moderator. How large a role the moderator plays depends on the size and complexity of the site. Powazek (p. 101) recommends small, compactly organized, and narrowly focused communities—which sound very much like the real-world, New Urbanist-style communities—in which the role of the moderator is abridged. A smaller community lends itself more manageably to self-rule.

Metaphorically speaking, instead of dealing with a city of millions of people moving around on foot, in taxis, on buses, and in cars talking to each other on land lines and fax machines, on cell phones, and by screaming at each other  from vehicles and on the street...we can choose to establish a village or neighborhood of people who are able to walk to see one another within a few minutes' time and communicate with each other by leaning out their windows or by meeting each other on someone's front porch or at the post office or on the village square. If all residents know each other and understand the community norms, they are much less likely to behave or speak in unacceptable ways or to require mediation of disagreements. They can work things out on their own. Of course, the neighborhood association or town council still exists, but their roles become much smaller and less important.

Principle 9: Cultivate a sense of accountability, continuity, and flow. Explaining how to operationalize this principle is as difficult as explaining how people fall in love. Without anyone dictating these qualities, it will become apparent whether or not a community has developed them. It must come from within the nature of the developing community itself. Whether or not the members are anonymous, any one member should be able to alert the others to someone's dishonesty or incivility or any other quality or behavior that does not live up to the group's norms. The members force the "sinner" to be accountable, own up to his/her transgressions, and change or they can boot the incorrigible one from the premises.

Continuity and flow are qualities that are recognized over time. They are primarily concerned with the

Susan Huelsing Sarapin

 dynamics of the interpersonal relationships and how they are manifested throughout the ongoing conversation. They can be inferred through a reading of the archives and over a specified period of time in the present. The two attributes work in concert to make the experience exciting, engaging, and relevant to its members, new or old. Turner (1982) would probably attribute a great deal of the flow of a community to the presence of communitas:

When the mood, style, or "fit" of spontaneous communitas is upon us, we place a high value on personal honesty, openness, and lack of pretensions or pretentiousness. We feel that it is important to relate directly to another person as he presents himself in the here-and-now, to understand him in a sympathetic way, free from the culturally defined encumbrances of his role, status, reputation, class, caste, sex, or other structural niche. Individuals who interact with one another in the mode of spontaneous communitas become totally absorbed into a single synchronized, fluid event (p. 48).

These qualities cannot be forced upon the community, but they will evolve into the essence of the community. If either or both become disrupted, the moderator can and should step in to set them back on track. Continuity and flow will emerge as the site's personality that infuses the community's purpose, and how they are perceived will determine who joins, who remains, who leaves, and ultimately, how vibrant and viable the community becomes.

The Chief Principle and Mechanisms of Community Evaluation

Principle 10: Evaluations of community sociability and usability must be conducted during its development, soon after launch, and at specified times throughout the community's evolution in order to assess the members' needs and if they are being fulfilled, and to predict the community's chances at success (Preece, p. 301). If one could select just one principle from all of the ones delineated in this paper, this could easily be considered the most critical to the ongoing success of a community. It is the principle that recognizes the inevitability of human error and the unpredictability of human behavior. A developer can plan to the nth degree for the best in intuitive usability and unfettered, democratic, egalitarian sociability, and still witness yet another failure of a group of people to morph into a community. According to Baym (1998), "It may not be possible to specify the specific factors that will combine to affect CMC outcomes in a particular group in advance of actual interaction, let alone what the impact of those factors will be" (p. xx). However, by defining benchmarks for success along the way, and taking the time and effort to evaluate various aspects of the community as a living, breathing organism, any part of the design, functional framework, or policies can be tweaked to better facilitate the growth and viability of the community.

There are numerous qualitative and quantitative measures available for conducting assessments of a variety of variables associated with the dynamics of online interpersonal communication. The ones selected for use will be determined by the goals of the evaluation and end-user of the results. Developers assess for the

Susan Huelsing Sarapin

 purpose of influencing the community's evolution; managers are interested in the financial or business impact of the group; and researchers evaluate to answer basic research questions (Preece, p. 303). This paper assumes the developer's position.

Developers typically use observation and interviews or surveys to obtain information about user needs and to verify that user requirements have been addressed and fulfilled as thoroughly as possible (Preece, p. 309). Infrastructure and software requirements are more related to the technical side of the community equation, so that will not be discussed here in our discourse about sociability despite the fact that objective usability is a much easier factor to measure than is the more subjective member satisfaction. Because statistical significance is not the aim of a developer's assessment, the number of members interviewed or surveyed does not carry the import that it does in a researcher's evaluation (Preece, p. 310). Generally speaking, the more members questioned, the better; the more frequently the evaluations are conducted, the better.

Open-ended questions related to sociability within a community could include the following:

1. Can I express myself in the manner I choose? If not, why not?

2. Do I feel that my contributions are being accepted nonjudgmentally? If not, why not?

3. Is the moderator doing a good job of keeping the conversation on topic? If not, what do you think should be changed?

4. Are the rules and policies clearly stated and easily found on the site? If not, how can we improve this situation?

5. What policies or protocols do you think should be added or deleted?

6. Do you find the discourse to be primarily civil and respectful? If not, what do you think we should do about this?

7. Do you like being a member of this community? If so, why? If not, why not?

8. How long have you been a member of this community and why have you remained a member?

9. Why did you join this community? Under what circumstances do you think you would leave?

There are many other questions that could be asked, and they should be asked if their answers could lead to improvements in the quality of the social interaction. The enhancements may be related to the content, the perceived maintenance and support of the original goals, new trends, etc., but the sociability function is directly related to the usability function, so this interconnection should be seriously reviewed as well. By observing and evaluating traffic, the number and frequency of postings, and the messages themselves, other factors can be measured in more quantitative ways. Again, the methods that are employed will be dictated by the type of information wanted.

The time may one day come to make the decision to "kill" a community. The possible reasons for doing such a thing are many, but the final decision to do it and the chosen method for accomplishing this must be thoroughly and critically considered. After all, the community actually belongs to its members, and they should be included in the decision-making process.

VIRTUAL SOCIABILITY

Susan Huelsing Sarapin

Conclusion

This paper has laid out 10 major principles for building, maintaining, and evaluating online communities. One could easily posit 20 or even 30 such principles. Distilling these to only 10 was a difficult exercise, but I think the 10 "commandments" listed and explicated here are crucial if one hopes to imagine, initiate, invest, insure, and influence a thriving community. No matter how skillful one is at planning for every conceivable event in the life of a virtual community, just as in the real world, its inhabitants will define it and direct its course. In some curious and enigmatic way, it will forever bear the mark of every person who ever sat down for a spell on its front porch.

References

Baym, N. (1998). The emergence of on-line community. In S. Jones (Ed.), Cybersociety 2.0 (pp. 35-68). Thousand Oaks: Sage.

Congress for the New Urbanism (2006). Retrieved November 15, 2006 from http://www.cnu.org/about/disp_faq.html

Figallo, C. (1993). The WELL: Small town on the Internet highway system. San Francisco, CA: Electric Frontier Foundation. Retrieved October 15, 2006 from http://www.eff.org/Net_culture/Virtual_community/well_figallo.article

Gefter, A. (2006). This is your space. New Scientist, 191, 46-48.

Gordon, L. & Gordon, C. (Producers), & Robinson, P. A. (Director). (1989). Field of Dreams [Motion picture]. United States: Universal Studios.

Ling, K., Beenen, G., Ludford, P., Wang, X., Chang, K., Li, X., . . . Kraut, R. (2005). Using social psychology to motivate contributions to online communities. Journal of Computer-Mediated Communication, 10(4), article 10. Retrieved November 18, 2006 from http://jcmc.indiana.edu/vol10/issue4/ling.html

McMillan, D. W., & Chavis, D. M. (1986). Sense of community: A definition and theory. Journal of Community Psychology, 14, 6-23. Retrieved November 16, 2006 from http://www.wam.umd.edu/~stwright/psych/sense-of-community.html

Powazek, D. M. (2002). Design for community: The art of connecting real people in virtual places. Indianapolis, IN: New Riders.

Preece, J. (2000). Online communities: Designing usability, supporting sociability. West Sussex, England: John Wiley & Sons.

Rheingold, H. (1993). The virtual community: Homesteading on the electronic frontier (Rev. ed.). Cambridge, MA: MIT Press.

Ridings, C. M., & Gefen, D. (2004). Virtual community attraction: Why people hang out online. Journal of Computer-Mediated Communication, 10(1). Retrieved November 18, 2006 from http://jcmc.indiana.edu/vol10/issue1/ridings_gefen.html

Smit, L. (2006). The ambiguity of community: New Urbanism's "sense of community" and its relation to social research. Urban Altruism. Calvin College.

The Village Tannin. Retrieved on November 16, 2006 from http://www.villagetannin.com/

Turner, V. (1982). From ritual to theater: The human seriousness of play. New York: Performing Arts Journal Publications.

Walther, J. B., & Parks, M. R. (2002). Cues filtered out, cues filtered in: Computer-mediated communication and relationships. In M. L. Knapp & J.

VIRTUAL SOCIABILITY

Susan Huelsing Sarapin

A. Daly (Eds.), Handbook of interpersonal communication (3rd ed., pp. 529-563). Thousand Oaks, CA: Sage.

Weinberger, D. (2002). Small pieces loosely joined. A unified theory of the web. Cambridge, MA: Perseus Publishing.

Wellman, B. (2001). Physical place and cyberplace: The rise of personalized networks. International Journal of Urban and Regional Research, 25(2), 227-252.

Wenger, E., McDermott, R., & Snyder, W. (2002). Cultivating communities of practice: A guide to Managing Knowledge. Boston, MA: Harvard Business School Press.

Wright, S. (n.d.). Psychological Sense of Community: Theory of McMillan & Chavis (1986). Retrieved November 16, 2002 from http://www.wam.umd.edu/~stwright/psych/sense-of-community.html

Glimpses of Community on the Web

Pamela Morris

http://ubimark.com/in/books/580/

Abstract
The application of the word 'community' in the online world has triggered rich discussion about just what community is and whether it can be achieved via the Internet. Various conceptions of community are revealed through a brief examination of current and past online groups such as the WELL and blogs, as well as the thoughts of a few current scholars. Along the way, several ideas for the application of community in the online world and related research are presented.

The term 'community' has been appropriated to describe the dynamics of interaction in online places. Experts have attempted to define what an online community is and what it is not, but it has proven difficult to capture a concept that is continually evolving and liberally applied, resulting in a term whose use is contentious both online and offline. When an online group is called 'community,' its members have different expectations of the group depending on their experience and beliefs about what community is and should be. The use of the term can even determine the evaluation of success or failure of that group. If one adheres to a traditional definition of community, then one may lament the demise of community both in society and on the Web. Some critics have said that the Internet can only provide the illusion of community. On the other hand, conceptualizations of community that allow room for fluid and loosely bound relationships,

Pamela Morris

 and even communities that are constructed by the individual, allow modern online and offline groups to make a claim for community. Online groups exemplify diverse characteristics that could contribute to such an updated definition of community.

Community, traditionally defined, is life lived in association with others, a society of unity of purpose or common interests often defined by geographical boundaries. Community includes social intercourse; fellowship and communion, shared values, and even common ownership (Oxford English Dictionary, 2007). Most online groups (and many of today's offline groups) are not communities per the traditional definition, and critics say the use of this definition is overly restrictive. The romanticized version of traditional community may have never existed, or, at least, has not existed for some time. The utopian, emotionally involved community sought by the WELL founders is likewise outdated, because the ontology of online community is "quite different from older social formations" (Matei, 2001, p. 8). As society changes, so does the notion of community, and this happened long before the advent of the Internet (Rheingold, 2000, pp. 346-347). New definitions of communities which are loosely formed and centered upon the individual more accurately describe many online and offline groups today. Comparing online interaction with various definitions of community can still be useful when evaluating online social constructions such as blogs and Wikipedia, and can be used to describe their successes and failures. Weinberger (2002) observed: "Because the web is fond of taking social structures, pounding them to bits, and letting the pieces rejoin themselves, groups, fundamental social units, are reinventing themselves in ways that challenge every assumption about groups in the real world" (p. 97). Any definition of community must therefore be applied with caution.

Building a sense of community is a worthy goal for shared online places, but the Web has not, from its earliest origins, been able to recapture traditional community. In 1985, a group of idealistic individuals founded an online place called the WELL (Whole Earth 'Lectronic Link). The WELL was a "second-chance incarnation of the countercultural communal movement" (Matei, 2001, p. 5). Many of its founders hoped to recapture what they felt had been lost in real life; a traditional sense of community among emotionally invested individuals. They felt that there was a "hunger for community that grows in the breasts of people around the world as more and more informal public spaces disappear from our real lives" (Rheingold, 1993, p. xx). These former counterculturists had tried once before to find the lost sense of community through communes; the effort failed. Likewise the original WELL ideals did not survive in a society that increasingly values the individual over community. However, the WELL is still vitally important to understanding the evolution of "community" online.

The WELL may have been closer to traditional community than any other online group both in attributes and expectations. This was largely because the original WELL was very unlike most online groups today. It was composed of people who were actually geographically close to one another and could have strong face-to-face relationships in addition to online ones. Rheingold (1993) said "it felt like an authentic

Pamela Morris

 community because it was grounded in the everyday physical world" (p. xvi). For some members, the WELL was just a supplemental form of communication between people who knew each other in real life. It was a small, tightly knit group that was generally left-leaning, valued quality discourse, and had a longing for a lost sense of togetherness. In his book, Rheingold stresses emotional investment and social interaction in his definition of community. "Virtual communities are social aggregations that emerge from the Net when enough people carry on [those] public discussions long enough, *with sufficient human feeling*, to form webs of personal relationships in cyberspace" (p. xx, italics added). He initially found in the WELL a "cozy little world" where people felt passionately about their online interactions (p. xv). He even said that his "sense of family on a fundamental level has been virtualized" (p. xxv). Throughout his book, Rheingold incorporates narratives exemplifying the intense level of emotional involvement of the WELL, from rallies of support for the parents of an ill child to round-the-clock efforts to find medical care for a traveling WELL member.

Seabrook also wrote about the WELL, and hints that the WELL was less than ideal. Most notably he struggled through the ranks of the WELL's elite, finally becoming "indoctrinated" into it. We see in Seabrook's (1993) stories the power of individual egos and the elitism of those in power begin to emerge; he states that "although the WELL was an excellent place to talk about democracy, it wasn't a democracy itself" (p. 186). Seabrook referred to the WELL as a dysfunctional family, where he observed that the "demand for self-expression engulfs the declared ideal of harmony, [and]

community spirit is drowned by self-absorbed competition for attention" (Matei, 2001, p. 22). The WELL failed to meet its objectives for several major reasons. First, it was trying to implement a sense of community which  no longer existed in society. This concept of community was familiar to the WELL's core membership but was largely inaccessible to others. Second, when the membership and ownership of the WELL changed, the core members were unwilling to allow their definition of community to evolve. The core membership could not reconcile with ownership that was impersonal, for-profit, and reshaped the WELL without the input or approval of core members. As membership grew, members could not maintain close emotional ties to a majority of other members. Many new participants chose to simply be observers, were not geographically near the WELL's nucleus, and did not participate in the face-to-face events. Rheingold (2000) later wrote that the WELL changed from a "little one-horse virtual community into a notorious cyberopolis" (p. 324).

The virtual community, or any modern community, is filled with tension between the needs of the individual and the needs of the community (Matei, 2001). The WELL was seeking a strong sense of community, and failed. Some think that community will succeed if it instead solves this tension in favor of individuality. Such communities are described as personalized networks by Wellman (2001) and hyperlinked organizations in *Cluetrain Manifesto* (Levine, Locke, Searls, & Weinberger, 2001).

Wellman's personal networks are created based on self-interest and the individual controls what groups are joined with what level of involvement. Although he

Pamela Morris

 avoids the use of the term community, Wellman (2001) defines it but says that it is supplied "separately to each individual. It is the individual, and neither the household nor the group, that is the primary unit of connectivity" (p. 238). These groups have permeable boundaries, interactions with diverse others, and connections that switch between multiple networks as well as membership that is voluntary and selective (Wellman, 2001). Such characteristics and choices are not a common part of traditional communities bounded by family or geography. They are also not unique to groups on the Internet; "the proliferation of personal networks happened well before the development of cyberspace" (Wellman, 2001, p. 228) and are found throughout modern society. Wellman gives examples of such personalized networks in governments and in modern organizational management. The writers of *The Cluetrain Manifesto* describe individualized online networks as having empowered communities that were once the helpless recipients of mass-market, mass-media messages and helpless to respond. Such groups, now connected, have re-established a voice. New communities are found where there were none before (for example, in hyperlinked organizations).

Calling a personalized network a community requires modifications to the definition of community. They are made of weak rather than strong ties, relationships are increasingly superficial, and leaving a network often has few consequences. In fact, Wellman (2001) notes that "these relationships are between fragments of selves, rather than between whole selves" (p. 244). One of Wellman's colleagues criticized the personalized network, saying "I think you are a wild eyed optimist to

think that 'person-to-person' networks are 'just as good as, if not better than' old-fashioned [...] networks...you surely cannot think that the two sorts of network are 'essentially identical'" (Wellman, 2001, p. 242). Of course online communities do not have geographical boundaries, but an online community could be delineated if the members and non-members are separated by some boundary. Unfortunately, online communities are not neatly bounded; they are fluid with members joining and leaving and being members of different communities simultaneously.

Communities of personalized networks are individually constructed, and are seen very differently by each member. Rheingold alluded to this in a post where he said "*I* find a community here for myself, and I don't believe that it is necessary for everybody else to agree for my sense of community to be valid" (as cited in Matei, 2001, p. 17). An online community can be "a subjective entity to be evaluated in terms of 'what matters to me'" (Matei, 2001, p. 19). As John Coate said "I like to say that if you think you are in a community you probably are, and if you don't, you aren't" (as cited in Matei, 2001, p. 18). Although allowing every definition to be equally valid may be a popular and inclusive way to define community, it is far too unrestrictive because it becomes difficult for anyone to determine the community boundaries, rules, and members. A myriad of communities of one does not seem particularly useful for defining a social gathering place. Coate ends his statement by noting that "the online environment lends itself well to a person who wants to [...] (be) completely disengaged from any

Pamela Morris

 sense of belonging to a community" (as cited in Matei, 2001, p. 18).

The blogosphere and Wikipedia are perhaps only marginally communities by any definition. They have been described as lawless or anarchistic, and are not only based on self-interest, but also on self-promotion. They have even been commoditized. Fitting such groups into any definition of community is extremely difficult, because as Weinberger (2002) explained, "the Web has kicked down most of the fencing that lets us recognize a group as a group" (p. 113). Further, "the laxness of many Web groups about membership can make them as coherent and persistent as the passing lane of a highway" (p. 112). In such uncommitted communities, "being a member does not obligate one to act in any certain way except to participate in some interaction. One certainly does not have to give up one's autonomy to be a part of a community" (Matei, 2001, p. 19).

Blogs are an extreme form of an individually-centered community. A blog consists of an individual (the blogger) and those people who for whatever reason are interested in that individual and the content of the blog. They are very loosely joined and, with the exception of the blogger, leaving such a community has almost no effect. The blogger has complete control of the main content and many times also has control over who participates in conversations about that content. Furthermore, participants (and bloggers) are not necessarily required to identify themselves and are allowed to use pseudonyms or participate anonymously. In this way, the sense in which you know someone online is often very different than in the real world. Weinberger (2002) gives a good description of an individual in the blogosphere: "what I know of him is what he chooses to show. I know him through what he has to say. I know him through the particularities of his page. I know him through his interests, [...] what he  wants to make public" (p. 103). It has also been repeatedly pointed out that the majority of blog (and Wikipedia) contributions come from a small part of the population (Schiff, 2006); they are certainly not egalitarian. A stand-alone blog tends to have a single author, a narrow focus and small audience, so small advertisers are seldom interested in a single blog. (Madden, 2005). A great many of these 'community' participants are simply observers (lurkers) there for information only or to be entertained. Others are unable to find or even enter this "community" at all. Blogs are the province of "a rather narrow and very privileged slice of the polity--those who are educated enough to take part in the wired conversation, who have the technical skills, and who are affluent enough to have the time and equipment." We are leaving these people behind in the new economy; everyday people are outside the conversation (Gillmor, 2004).

Some claim that blogs and Wikipedia do have some characteristics of a traditional community. The host of InstaPundit claims that "blogs are reproducing something people thought for a long time we had lost, the discussion in the public sphere by the ordinary people" (Kornblum, 2003). A Wired magazine reporter wrote that Howard Dean's astronomically popular Meetup blog "on the foundation of a new technology, [...] revived an outdated form," that of a traditional political community (Wolf, 2004). Whether or not Wikipedia is a community depends upon how deeply

VIRTUAL SOCIABILITY

Pamela Morris

one looks at it. On the surface, it claims to be all-inclusive by being editable by anyone, any time. The pooling of wisdom used to create the knowledge capital of Wikipedia and other crowdsourced efforts is an old concept, used by communities throughout time. A New Yorker writer said: "perhaps Wikipedia's greatest achievement [...] was the creation of a community," and called it a utopian project (Schiff, 2006). Behind the entries are passionate individuals who are "compulsively social," carrying on conversations and philosophizing. The motivation to participate actively is largely voluntary, unpaid, and therefore often stems from a passion not unlike that of the WELL's early members. Some say that the primary motivation in the newest types of online groups is simply the pleasure of online work.

However, Wikipedia as a community has many critics, co-founder Larry Sanger chief among them. Critics argue that the lawlessness and free-for-all cannot work. There is much anonymity among Wikipedia participants, and quite a bit of negative posting. Although conversation happens behind the scenes, the main content is not supposed to be original thought, but just presentation of facts. Entries are to be neutral and cited, and argument about the content likewise (if it is to ever contribute to the entry). Wikipedia claims to be egalitarian, but is in reality structured (although according to critics, not yet enough or in the right way). "What began as an experiment in unfettered democracy, has sprouted policies and procedures" and become a "regulatory thicket" (Schiff, 2006). The hierarchy needed because "even online democracy has its limits" (McHenry, 2004). Not all participants are equal, instead "the user who spends the most time on the site – or who

yells the loudest – wins" and there is no
privilege to those who know what
they're talking about (Schiff, 2006). The
motivation of Wikipedia contributors is
questionable; it has been called "a dash
of altruism, a dose of obsessive
compulsiveness, and good chunk of egotism" (Goetz,
2003), and it has been called "the world's most
ambitions vanity press" (Schiff, 2006).

Online groups such as blogs and Wikipedia have
become increasingly mediated and commodified. These
communities are often neither self-forming nor self-
sustaining. According to Rheingold's (2000) later
writing, healthy online communities need guidance and
"action must be taken to glue people together" (p. 341).
They require skilled facilitation, well-thought-out social
contracts, and social mechanisms. In addition, many
online places are becoming commercialized. For
example, blogs have been used as marketing tools and
even hosted (and controlled by) by corporations on
behalf of both consumers and employees. Although the
audience of commodified blogs theoretically has the
ability to 'talk back,' the writers of the *Cluetrain
Manifesto* would probably be suspicious of such tight
corporate control. Making money from community is
certainly not compatible with either the traditional or
individual flavors of community. Rheingold (2000) asks,
"In America, the idea of public property has grown
increasingly unfashionable. [...] Is there still space in
cyberspace for public property [...]?" (p. 379)

Conclusion

"Virtual communities might be real communities, they
might be pseudocommunities, or they might be
something entirely new in the realm of social contracts,"

Pamela Morris

 (Rheingold, 2000, p. 362). On one hand, those who insist on traditional definitions hold that online groups are only pseudocommunities and online interaction is only para-social. One critic said "pseudocommunity is a reversal of a centuries old trend from organic community based on personal relationships, to impersonal associations integrated by mass means" (Rheingold, 2000, p. 349). Others, myself included, believe that modern definitions of community are needed. For example, artificially created task-oriented communities such as those created by corporations for employees could be allowed to call themselves a community so that they may experience the perceived advantages of that social structure. Further, there is a need to allow multiple definitions of because "there is no such thing as a single monolithic online subculture; it's more like an ecosystem of subcultures, some frivolous, others serious" (Rheingold, 1993, p. xviii).

Although it is tempting to try to define community, this paper did not attempt to do that. Instead, it showed how an examination of past and current online groups can help shape what "community" means both online and offline. The explosive growth of the Internet has created a proliferation of virtual communities, and the nature of those communities is diverse. The Web has the "ability to evolve new forms so rapidly that if real-world evolution worked as fast, we could move from grapefruit to squid in a couple of months" (Weinberger, 2002, p. 113). The definition of community must evolve to some extent, or it will no longer apply to any existing group. How much that definition could and should change is a fertile area of discussion among psychologists, sociologists and communication scientists, because "developing technologies are creating an expended social environment that requires amendments and alterations to way in which we conceptualize social processes" (Rheingold, 2000, pp. 366-367).

References

community. (2007). In Oxford English Dictionary. Oxford University Press. Retrieved from Purdue Library database.

Gillmor, D. (2004) We the media - grassroots journalism by the people, for the people. Introduction. Retrieved from http://www.authorama.com/we-the-media-1.html

Goetz, T. (2003). Open source everywhere. Wired Magazine 11(11), November 2003. Retrieved from http://www.wired.com/wired/archive/11.11/opensource.html?pg=1&topic=&topic_set=

Kornblum, J. (2003, July 8). Welcome to the blogosphere. USA Today. Retrieved from http://www.usatoday.com/tech/webguide/internetlife/2003-07-08-blogs_x.htm

Levine, R., Locke, C., Searls, D., & Weinberger, D. (2001). The cluetrain manifesto. New York: Perseus.

Madden, A. P. (2005, August). The business of blogging. Technology Review, 36-38. Retrieved from http://www.technologyreview.com/Biztech/14653/?a=f

Matei, S. (2001). From counterculture to cyberculture. Virtual community discourse and the dilemma of modernity. Retrieved from http://www.matei.org/learn/cybertheory/pdfs/counterculture-cyberculture.pdf.

VIRTUAL SOCIABILITY

Pamela Morris

McHenry, R. (2004, November 15). The faith-based encyclopedia. TCS Daily. Retrieved from http://www.tcsdaily.com/article.aspx?id=111504A

Rheingold, H. (2000). The virtual community: homesteading on the electronic frontier (Rev. ed.). Cambridge, Mass.: MIT Press.

Rheingold, H. (1993). The Virtual Community: homesteading on the electronic frontier (1st HarperPerennial ed.). New York, NY: HarperPerennial.

Schiff, S. (2006, July 31) Know it all. The New Yorker. Retrieved from http://www.newyorker.com/archive/2006/07/31/060731fa_fact

Seabrook, J. (1997). Deeper. New York, NY: Simon & Schuster.

Weinberger, D. (2002). Small pieces loosely joined. New York: Perseus.

Wellman, B. (2001). Physical place and cyber place: the rise of personalized networks. International Journal of Urban and Regional Research, 25(2), 227-252.

Wolf, G. (2004). How the Internet invented Howard Dean. Wired Magazine, 12(1). Retrieved from http://www.wired.com/wired/archive/12.01/dean.html?pg=1&topic=&topic_set =

Peering Behind the Curtain: The Virtual Wizard Offers No Guarantees

Brenda Berkelaar

http://ubimark.com/in/books/581/

Abstract

This paper employs Maslow's hierarchy of needs as a starting point for examining the formation of online community. Setting current online sociability in the socio-historic context of the Internet, popular and scholar publications, and differing definitions of community, the author argues that the liminality of *communitas* is a more typical manifestation of online interaction than *community* per se. That being said, the individual-corporate tensions demonstrated and the need fulfillment possible do offer the potential for online community. Practical recommendations for effective online community design include appreciating the context, fundamental assumptions, and research that together increase the likelihood of, but do not guarantee, the emergence of authentic online community.

In *The Wizard of Oz* (Fleming, 1939*)*, the Scarecrow, the Cowardly Lion, the Tin Man, and Dorothy set off to the Emerald City in search of the wizard who they believe can meet their respective needs. Their reasons for traveling to the Emerald City are not much different from the reasons many people go online. People go online in search of knowledge (a brain), safe places, (courage, e.g., to explore their identity or practice interaction), social and emotional connections (a heart), and online communities (a home). Dorothy and her friends feel confident that the wizard will meet all their

Brenda Berkelaar

 needs. Unfortunately, they discover that the wizard is "a very good man but a bad wizard" (Fleming, 1939), and therefore is not the savior promised. Although the wizard meets some of their needs – the Scarecrow gets a brain, the Cowardly Lion, courage, and the Tin Man, a heart – Dorothy's return to her home, to community, remains elusive until she realizes she must click the heels of her ruby slippers and chant "There's no place like home. There's no place like home."

The Internet is a virtual Oz, promising Emerald Cities with benevolent wizards where people will connect and fulfill their needs. Relatively new and rapidly developing Internet phenomena, online sociability, and online "communities" provide opportunities to meet but not guarantee some of these basic human psychosocial needs. Although it does not provide the unabridged script, this paper will introduce the basic plot and some of the main characters associated with online sociability research and conceptions of virtual or online communities.

While finding a unifying thread in scholarly discourse, or any discourse about online sociability presents a challenge, it seems apparent that online sociability and online "community" are about more than they initially appear (Matei, 2001; Rheingold, 1993, 2000; Seabrook, 1997; Weinberger, 2002; Wellman, 2001). Like any human endeavor, online sociability is complex. One of the challenges of researching online sociability is making the invisible aspects visible—to see, as it were, the wizard behind the curtain.

And that is the thing about life. You go walking along, thinking people are talking a language and exchanging ideas, but the whole time there is this deeper language people are really talking, and that language has nothing to do with ethics, fashion, or politics, but what it really has to do with is feeling important and valuable. (Miller, 2004, p. 45)

In 1943, humanist psychologist Abraham Maslow introduced his famous hierarchy of human needs, expanded later in his book *Motivation and Personality* (1954). In his now classic theory, Maslow's hierarchy divides needs into two broad categories: (a) physical— which includes safety and physiological needs; and (b) psychosocial—which includes social needs (love/belonging), status/esteem, and self-actualization (Maslow, 1943, 1954). Naïve readings may see need fulfillment as a unilateral linear process; however the practical realization of Maslow's hierarchy is neither linear nor static. Rather need fulfillment is dynamic, with the dominant need always shifting and single behaviors sometimes incorporating multiple needs e.g. dining out with friends accomplishes both physical and social needs (Maslow, 1943, 1954). As well, some need fulfillment may require a level of reciprocity (i.e. social) since unilateral pursuit tends to undermine relational interaction.

Initially enjoying wide acceptance, Maslow's hierarchy has been challenged (Wahba & Bridwell, 1976). Reviews of needs research suggest that needs are not necessarily established as a hierarchy (Wahba & Bridwell, 1976); however, few would argue that humans have basic physical and psychosocial needs. In the same way that Freud focused our attention on the importance of the unconscious, Maslow's work was

Brenda Berkelaar

 valuable in highlighting humanity's psychosocial needs, needs that may be filled by online interactions.

Even if one ignores the hierarchical relationship between Maslow's needs, his framework can provide a starting point from which to view online sociability. Since the Internet is a non-physical place, Maslow's two physical needs (physical safety and physiological) are not (or rather not as obviously) applicable to online sociability as discussed here; however work on the nature of embodiment and safety online, not discussed here, might find value in exploring the nature of physical safety online. Maslow's three psychosocial needs particularly: (a) love/belonging, (b) status (esteem), and (c) self-actualization/transcendence speak to some of the background motivations and foundations for online sociability. For Maslow, the need for love and belonging requires that people have the opportunity give and receive love and belong to a group or a community. The need for esteem requires self-respect and respect from others, and finally, the need for self-actualization involved the realization of the potentiality with the individual (Maslow, 1943, 1954). Online environments promise and may (or may not) provide means to fulfill some or all of these needs for people, and not necessarily in the order Maslow predicted.

Not every technology offers the promise of psychosocial need fulfillment like the Internet. For example, the telephone does not as easily provide access to the size of audience or particular types of people that might provide a sense of belonging or status, particularly for those in very narrowly defined groups. If you are a "black sheep" within your local community, electronic bulletin boards, chatrooms, and

UseNets allow you to connect with people with similar interests (Rheingold, 1993, 2000; Wellman, 2001) and provide a place to belong. It offers an environment in which one can explore and develop one's identity(ies)  (Matei, 2001). Wikipedia offers the opportunity to teach the world your specific knowledge (Sanger, 2005; Schiff, 2006) and in doing so build esteem. Some also argue the Web goes beyond individual or communitarian needs, but is a place to attempt to resolve tensions between individual identity (esteem and self-actualization/transcendence) and communal desires (social belonging) (Matei, 2001) allowing one perhaps to fulfill both needs simultaneously. The Internet, thus, offers the potential to fulfill a wide range of psychosocial needs.

Before going further, to truly understand online sociability one must have some sense of its socio-historical context. The Internet grew out of research initiated during the Cold War. In order to minimize vulnerability of attack on the information and technology systems, the Department of Defense created a distributed (rather than a centralized) network for sharing critical information. As a decentralized network, the system would be difficult to control or to destroy. In 1969, ARPANET (Advanced Research Projects Agency Network) transferred its first message. The ARPANET eventually evolved into what is now known as the Internet. Initially the domain of academic researchers, the Internet became privately available in the 1980s, and people began to use of the Internet for personal and social activities (Hauben & Hauben, 1999), prior to the deluge of commercialization epitomized in the dotcom era.

VIRTUAL SOCIABILITY

Brenda Berkelaar

 Thus, prior to the 1980s, computing was considered a non-social activity (S. Matei, personal communication, August 29, 2006); however, in 1985, some key individuals in the 1960s countercultural movement, Stewart Brand (author of the Whole Earth Catalog) and Larry Brilliant decided to prove that the computer offered a unique means for genuine human connection. The WELL, or the Whole Earth 'Lectronic Link, was a grand social experiment in online communities. The basic structure of the WELL was a gathering of like-minded, mostly men of a certain generation, from the 60s subculture, particularly Deadheads, in virtual space. The community "glue" of the WELL was their shared ideology, specifically that the Internet offered a viable means of achieving self-expression and self-discovery without sacrificing community (Matei, 2001).

The WELL was significant because it was one of the first and longest lasting virtual communities, making it one of the world's most influential online communities (Hafner, 1997). The WELL also avoided the complete anonymity available elsewhere on the Web, requiring that people subscribe using their real name, and archiving posts. (A comprehensive and dynamic account of its history is available in Katie Hafner's *The Epic Saga of the Well*, Hafner, 1997). Divided by subject areas into conferences, the WELL was a text-based bulletin-board, providing a contemporary salon for discussion and exploration of topics of interest. Hafner's *Saga* alludes to the influence of the 60s countercultural movement on the WELL. In addition to Brand and Brilliant, other members of the 60s countercultural movement were hired as directors throughout its life and many of its early and core members were ex-hippies (Hafner, 1997; Matei, 2001; Rheingold, 1993, 2000; Seabrook, 1997).

Along with Hafner's *Saga* (1997), two key books critical to understanding the significance of the WELL and early online communities are Howard Rheingold's *Homesteading on the Virtual Frontier* (1993, 2000) and John Seabrook's *Deeper* (1997). Through the lens of Maslow's hierarchy, and with the provocative narratives and commentaries of Rheingold and Seabrook, one easily can imagine Wellites pursuing self-actualization and a sense of belonging through their online WELL experiences, albeit not always in the most artful or successful ways possible.

An ex-hippie, Howard Rheingold coined the term "virtual community" in his seminal work *The Virtual Community: Homesteading on the Electronic Frontier* (1993, 2000). Rheingold's book significantly shaped the way the mainstream public conceives of virtual communities (S. Matei, personal communication, August 31, 2006). In *Homesteading*, Rheingold shares his personal experiences on the WELL, those of other community members (called *pern*), and his reflections, all of which imply a relatively utopian view of the Internet. Internet technology offered the potential to connect the knowledge of individuals through the development of a "group mind" of shared knowledge and to connect people emotionally and socially (Rheingold, 1993). The WELL community was glued together with "social network capital, knowledge capital, and communion" (p. xxviii). *Homesteading* offers someone new to the area an introduction to the earliest days of online community. Even with addition of a

VIRTUAL SOCIABILITY

Brenda Berkelaar

 retrospective, Rheingold remains a firm believer in the promise of virtual space for people's self-actualization and social connection in spite of some negative experiences. Despite its origins in the Department of Defense, and his caveats about the potential negative aspects of the Internet, Rheingold sees the Internet as offering great potential to humanity, if only we engage in significant research and work to create community (Rheingold, 2000, p. 390).

In contrast, journalist John Seabrook's *Deeper* (1997) provides the perspective of an outsider who initially lurked (observed) at the WELL while researching an article. Taunted by active WELL members, Seabrook's initiation and participation within the WELL moved beyond two initial articles to the development of a book. Seabrook's account of the WELL is less positive than Rheingold's proto-utopia, providing a counterpoint, or at least some constraints on Rheingold's perspective. In his descriptions, Seabrook (1997) implies that the WELL is a dysfunctional family, a place for the performance of identity, and a Freudian boiling pot of pressure. Although Seabrook (1997) did not have the overwhelming positive response to the WELL as Rheingold, he uncovered some key aspects of virtual community, such as hazing behaviors and the complicated difficult-to learn keyboard-based interface, practices acknowledged by Rheingold as some of the ritual and rites for the WELL community.

Maslow proposed that all individuals need a sense of belonging or social connection (Maslow, 1943, 1954) something traditionally offered by a community. Rheingold (1993) describes virtual communities as "social aggregations that emerge from the NET when enough people carry on those public discussions long enough, with sufficient human feeling to form webs of personal relationships in cyberspace" (p. xxi).  Some people see this idea of *"virtual community* as a perversion of the notion of community" (Rheingold, 2000, p. 325). In his book *Silicon Snake Oil*, Cliff Stoll (1996), a former WELLite, dismisses virtual community as an empty imitation of real community (as cited in Rheingold, 2000, p. 327); however, in reading Rheingold's and Seabrook's WELL narratives with all their complexity, emotion, and interaction, it is hard to not "sense" community. When WELLites come together with "beams" (virtual positive emotions), information or digital contact for a member suffering a life-threatening illness overseas, the intangibility of community seems tangible. How can one measure or evaluate community whether it exists digitally or physically? When asked, most people could not necessarily define community but would "know it when they see it". Community seems tangible to many people – in a physical sense – even if one can't exactly put a finger on it. People know when they "belong" and when they don't.

One problem in recognizing virtual community is the fact that the Internet as a whole seems to have many nonexamples of community; that is, every site which declares itself a community is not in fact a community, and some sites exist simply for individual consumption or presentation. That is, they might better fill different psychosocial needs or some other need altogether. Online, community is often a marketing term. So then, what is an acceptable indicator(s) for community? Is true community fundamentally face-to-face (f2f), as implied by many common criticisms of virtual life? If

Brenda Berkelaar

 community requires f2f, it follows that many of the technologies we use to connect with people are also inherently limiting to community development, including telephones, letters, and others. So if not f2f, how then do we measure community or at least determine whether it exists online or off?

The Internet provides a relatively new venue for human interaction, sociability, and community. New research areas often find it helpful to borrow research from other fields as starting points for understanding. Helpful overviews regarding the psycho-social aspects of online interaction exist (Kiesler, Siegel, & McGuire, 1984; Walther & Parks, 2002). For example, Kiesler et al.'s 1984 study highlights an overview of specific empirical research related to understanding the sociobehavioral aspects of online sociability with recommendations for future study. Walther and Parks' 2002 study provides a critical review of various theories used to help understand this online sociability. However, it is necessary to look beyond research on online interactions alone. Highly valuable for the researcher and the practitioner, anthropological and cultural theories of community provide a broad framework within which to understand and evaluate more specific details. If virtual, or digital, community is community, than to some degree it should perhaps reflect those essential components of community described within the social sciences, although perhaps reinterpreted for the particular context and approach of online interactions.

In the 1890s, sociologist Ferdinand Toennies distinguished between the sociological categories of (1988) community (*gemeinschaft*) and society (*gesellschaft*). Written during the Industrial Revolution, Toennies problematized the idea of community versus society given the increase in individualization. According to Toennies, gemeinschaft was regulated  by common mores in which the individual primarily subsumes to the larger association. In contrast, with gesellschaft, the larger association never supersedes the individual and emphasis was placed on secondary relationship and elaborate divisions of labor. From perspective of Maslow's hierarchy, gesellschaft appears better suited to self-actualization while gemeinschaft encourages a greater sense of belonging. From a Toennian perspective, the Internet with its loose ties, heterogeneity, and physical distance at most seems to achieve gesellschaft (society) and lacks genuine gemeinschaft (community).

Communitas, a term reinterpreted by anthropologist Victor Turner, provides a unique perspective of the potential of the Internet to provide a place of belonging even if it is not necessarily community (gemeinschaft). While comprehensively described in Turner's book *The Ritual Process Structure and Anti-Structure* (1995), the key elements of Turner's concept of communitas and the associated liminality are clearly summarized in the Routledge *Encyclopedia of Religious Rites, Rituals, and Festivals* (Turner, 2004) and Mathieu Deflem's 1991 paper. Communitas refers to the "sense of sharing and intimacy that develops among persons who experience liminality as a group" (Turner, 2004, p. 97). In liminal space all are "treated equally, deprived of all distinguishing characteristics of social structure, constituting 'a community...of comrades and not a structure of hierarchically arranged positions'" (Turner,

Brenda Berkelaar

1967, as cited in Deflem, 1991). Communitas is community; however, Turner includes some significant caveats. Communitas arises as a *temporary* condition that critiques the existing social structure. "Communitas liberates individuals from conformity to general norms" (Turner, 2004, p. 98). More recently, Deflem refined the concept of liminality for the modern industrialized world (Deflem, 1991), referring to liminoid phenomena as particular manifestations of modern culture that challenge the existing structure.

Utilizing these cultural concepts of communitas and liminality, Barbatisis, Fegan, and Hansen (1999) highlight the 'betwixt and between' of cyberspace where someone can "be" in two places at once. People who engage in virtual interactions are "present in two realities simultaneously: one, a physical embodied presence...the other, a 'sense' of presence in an ideated or nonmaterial reality. Cyberspace, being liminal, becomes a 'place of possibility'" (Barabatsis et al., 1999, para. 1). The temporary and liminal nature of communitas, as opposed to community (gemeinschaft), better allows for the affective quality of interaction Rheingold uses to describe the WELL as a virtual community, while also allowing for countercultural ideals and the anonymity and deindividuation characteristics apparent in online interactions.

Given the distinction between community and communitas, the Internet can be more easily seen as a place for communitas (and liminality) rather than a place for community *per se*. This is not to say that community does not occur online, only that communitas is a more natural expression of the medium. This is particularly evident in its appropriation by the 60s

countercultural movement as a means to critique society and resolve issues with its current structure, to move toward equality rather than the competition of contemporary institutions. Seabrook (1997) refers to the WELL as:

A natural museum of the sixties...[with] the commune [as a] early controlling metaphor for understanding community life on the WELL...a cross between The Farm and Brook farm...[which was]... envisioned as 'a society of liberal, intelligent, and cultivated persons whose relations with each other would permit a more wholesome and simple life than can be led amidst the pressures of our competitive institutions' (p. 157).

Hafner also talks about the "lush promises [the Internet] whispered in our ear" (1997); however, it is Matei's (2001) article that truly highlights the countercultural aspect of the WELL, other virtual communities, and the Internet itself. For Matei, online sociability (and online community) is a new attempt to resolve the modern dilemma—the tension between the need for individuality and the need for community—the same dilemma that was the focus of the 60s countercultural movement. Virtual community is therefore, a subspecies of the counterculture (p. 6).

Matei (2001) sees the countercultural ideals of the WELL as fundamentally shaping virtual communities concluding that "virtual communities act both as solvent and glue in modern society" (p. 2). The advent of new technologies is often expected to fulfill two competing visions – vision "for greater autonomy and increased personal agency"... and "dreams of social harmony and

Brenda Berkelaar

 homogenization" (p. 3). In *From Counterculture to Cyberculture*, (Matei, 2001) highlights the key contradictions of individual and community as evidenced in virtual communities. In attempts to achieve a better society, the WELL, and other online communities, must deal with tensions between: "self-expression and community involvement, ascribed and achieved identities, intentional sociability and actional efficiency, and between strong and weak ties" (p. 5). The Internet promised "a new sense of community, where individuality is not repressed, but cultivated" (p. 10) allowing for simultaneous or corresponding fulfillment of the need to self-actualize and the need to belong. Matei highlights technology discourse that affirms the ability of the technology as uniquely able to provide a sense of equality among its users even as debates continue regarding the fundamental nature of the Internet community and its ability to genuinely provide a genuine solution to this modern dilemma.

In his own book *Small Pieces Loosely Joined* (Weinberger, 2002) and in his collaboration on *The Cluetrain Manifesto* (Locke, Levine, Searls, & Weinberger, 2001), Weinberger indirectly refers to the concepts of liminality and the 60's counterculture. Like Rheingold and Seabrook, Weinberger embeds personal experience in his discourse (Locke et al., 2001; Weinberger, 2002). One of the key concerns surrounding online sociability explored in Weinberger's chapters is the idea of human experience as embodied. The lack of physicality is of major concern for many online sociability critics (Kiesler et al., 1984; Walther & Parks, 2002). For Weinberger, embodiment matters because embodiment is our fundamental human condition; however, his sense of embodiment is not a strict sense of physicality but rather the actualization of experience as lived through the individual. Embodiment, to Weinberger is about having a voice. Life used to be a  spectator sport that provided certainty and security but lacked individuality (Weinberger, 2002). The Internet provided transcendence (one of Maslow's original needs) in a way that changed people's relationship with what was important and meaningful (S. Matei, personal conversation, September 21, 2006), i.e. companies flattened and connected in response to new philosophies from the 60s counterculture (Locke et al., 2001; Matei, 2001; Weinberger, 2002). The Internet to Weinberger is a conversation not a mass marketing piece (Weinberger, 2002). Individuals must present themselves as expressions of their interests as members of a newly shaped shared world in a sense self-actualizing through virtual means. "The Web is fond of taking social structures, pounding them to bits, and letting the piece rejoin themselves, groups – fundamental social units – are reinventing themselves in ways that challenge every assumption about groups in the real world" (p. 97). Community for Weinberger is individually focused, it is effectively "small pieces loosely joined".

How does one sort out this seeming paradox of individualized community as articulated by Weinberger? Look to Barry Wellman. To Wellman, community in the modern world is individual networks rather than traditional groups (Wellman, 2001). "Each person has his/her own 'personal community'" (para. 1). Specifically, "communities are transforming from solitary groups to individualized networks" (para. 3).

VIRTUAL SOCIABILITY

Brenda Berkelaar

 Community is therefore defined "spatially rather than socially" (para. 2). This expanded sense of social networks with its weak and strong ties is enabled by the networking capabilities of the Internet. Whereas previously communities were often bounded by physical space, the Internet removes that limitation, giving access to a broader variety of individuals. For Wellman, social networks are about providing *useful* connections (2001) more than about providing a sense of *belonging* that traditional community definitions highlight. Interestingly enough, in his postlogue, *Rethinking Virtual Communities*, Rheingold (2000) refers to Wellman's work, wishing he had known about it so he could have avoided the headache of the virtual community discussion by using the term social networks; however, it has been suggested that a book on social networks would not have quite the same marketing value as *Virtual Community: Homesteading on the Electronic Frontier* (S. Matei, personal conversation, September 21, 2006).

This shifting to emphasis on individualized networks (Weinberger, 2002; Wellman, 2001) and the tension between the individual and community are significant philosophical questions and assumptions underlying understandings of online sociability. They also imply a tension between self-actualization, esteem, and social need fulfillment. Further application of countercultural ideals and social networking to contemporary online communities, along with additional research, may reaffirm countercultural tensions and individual expression as fundamental to the nature of online communities or a component of the evolutionary process of cultural and social development – acting as liminal spaces before becoming altered versions of the initial structure, again requiring revision in the same way that the original 60s "counterculture has become a mainstream cultural movement" (Matei, 2001, p. 10).

The idea that countercultural assumptions exist both online and offline implies that the differentiation between real life and virtual life so often articulated within popular discourse is to some degree artificial. The two are not mutually exclusive. The term cyberspace comes from Gibson's (1984) *Neuromancer*. To Gibson, cyberspace was "a space apart from the corporeal world" (as cited in Agre, 1999, para. 1); however, Rheingold's (1993) personal experience integrates the two: "I inhabit my virtual communities... my virtual communities also inhabit my life" (p. xxv). In addition, socio-cultural research implies that many individuals use the Internet as one particular mode of interaction with others, and that many relationships initiated online eventually progress to offline interaction of varying types (Kiesler et al., 1984; Walther & Parks, 2002). This is not to say that they are the same, but rather that there is overlap, simply by the nature of both involving human socio-cultural and socio-psychological functions.

The disconnect between cyberspace and the corporeal world is part of the "cultural imagination" that has disserved us (Agre, 1999). In *Life After Cyberspace*, an early article on the false dichotomy of virtual life (VL) and real life (RL), Agre (1999) outlines contemporary user interface research that is blurring the boundaries between the computer-mediated world and the real world. Computers and the Internet are embedded more and more within social processes and social

Brenda Berkelaar

 relationships. In making VL and RL mutually exclusive people fail to appreciate the ways in which people use the Internet in complement with "a whole ecology of media" to develop their identities, their communities of practice, and to address their important matters. Finally, Agre (1999) wants us to appreciate the highly responsive and rapidly evolving nature of the Internet. As a result, the Internet, and "communities" on it should be at any point in time seen as "a snapshot in motion."

So where does this leave us?

Like many other socio-cultural constructs, the Internet is not an all or nothing deterministic entity but rather an evolving conglomeration of expectations, perceptions, and potentiality. The Internet provides potential, in a particularly unique way for the development of online sociability that allows for individualization and community connection; however, this potential is neither necessary nor sufficient. While Rheingold (2000) argues that the Internet and its supporting technology are not necessarily neutral (his optimistic assumptions are still evident in his postlogue *Rethinking Virtual Communities*, he believes people need to actively engage the tool to shape its course rather than being passively determined by it. Every technology has inherent advantages and limitations—it is the proper recognition of underlying assumptions, its advantages, and limitations, along with the proper application of the technology to a particular situation or problem that determines to some degree its inevitable success or failure, particularly as community or communitas.

While the Internet is not deterministically transformative, it has significant raw transformative potential. The phenomenon of blogging has allowed individuals to present themselves, to share their ideas, and to construct themselves in ways that were before not possible. In addition, blogs and other online communication tools  have demonstrated ability to make candidates viable, although not politically bulletproof. Howard Dean, a relative nobody on the political scene, unintentionally leveraged the political influence of the Internet, inventing himself (or rather having others invent him) as a viable presidential candidate (Wolf, 2004). As a result of the decentralization and relative ubiquity of the Internet, knowledge and credibility were redefined. Bloggers and Web authors with "a viewpoint, the ability to write, and a readership" (Weinberger, 2002, p. 122), yet lacking traditional qualifications, become experts and authorities. Authenticity is a central in the online context. Wikipedia allows anyone, within minimal guidelines, to share their knowledge, and teach the world (Sanger, 2005; Schiff, 2006). The Internet allows expertise, knowledge, and authority, to be removed, to some degree, from the hands of traditional experts—or at least to be created, produced, and delivered by those who formerly lacked an authoritative voice. Knowledge became a social phenomenon (Wenger, McDermott, & Snyder, 2002). Online environments can provide a place for people to develop esteem, explore their potential (self-actualization), and create a connection or sense of belonging with others.

In order to fulfill these potential needs, practically speaking, designers need to appreciate the context, fundamental assumptions, and research that can inform design. For example, although many sites are labeled as communities, the name is not sufficient to get people to

Brenda Berkelaar

 come, to stay, and to come back, in essence to be part of a community, rather than simply a visitor. As Preece (2000) recommends, the goal should be to support online sociability in an intentional way. Although her definition of community as getting people to come, to stay, and to come back, is relatively broad, Preece (2000) would appreciate two critical practical implications of this research: (a) online community and online sociability involve more than the presence of technology and people. There is no guarantee that having both will necessarily result in community, and (b) the particular technology and the particular people that form a virtual space influence online community and online sociability. The assumptions of the people and of the technology will come to the surface of the site eventually and either reinforce a particular sense of community or online sociability or undermine or even disallow the development of community or online sociability.

Assumptions matter. Good designers know what's going on behind the curtain. Designers must be aware both of the assumptions and expectations of the technology, of the users, and of themselves as they create their sites. This is not an easy task. To create connection or to provoke online sociability, designers must get people to come, get people to stay, and get people to come back. Unfortunately there is no clearly marked yellow brick road to follow. Still, some signposts exist.

When it comes to fulfilling socio-psychological needs, online sociability and virtual communities persist and exist because they continue to offer a way, a particularly unique way, to meet the psychosocial needs of contemporary humanity; however there is no guarantee. Even as they provide unique options for fulfilling personal psychosocial needs, online spaces also provide hindrances. Virtual environments can be deindividuating,  their very nature stripping away some of the elements of individual identity (Baym, 1998). The liminal potential of the space lends itself to temporary points of belonging and equality, but there temporary nature may not, and perhaps will not, satiate human needs. Additionally, given the burgeoning growth of social networks, what are the implications of large-scale individually-oriented networks as the definition of community – particularly those with weak ties – on one's sense of belonging. From the perspective of Maslow's hierarchy, the Internet offers some new ways to potentially meet socio-psychological needs, although it is not *the* way for all, or perhaps even some individuals.

There are still many unanswered questions and points of contention about online sociability and virtual communities. In resolving these one must consider tradeoffs, since there is rarely one right answer. How do we reconcile the value of anonymity to the anonymous, without increasing the risk to those at the wrong end of anonymity used badly (e.g. flaming)? What are the implications of fragmented and slippery identity online? What does it mean to have a virtually constructed identity? How is an online identity constructed differently than offline identity if at all? What about the problem of embodiment? How much does the physical really matter? What is the relative value of RL versus VL? Can it even be quantified in a generalizable way? What are the implications of increasing

VIRTUAL SOCIABILITY

Brenda Berkelaar

 commercialization and private ownership? Is community possible? Is it possible to find specific practical factors that increase the likelihood of high quality community or online socialization? How do we more effectively integrate research and practice? Most importantly, if community is indeed shifting toward individualized networks and "small pieces loosely joined" (Weinberger, 2002) what are the long-term implications? These and more questions along with the rapidly evolving nature of online sociability energize future research both theoretical and applied.

The Internet is not an Emerald City with a benevolent wizard—there may be semblances of Emerald Cities and people claiming wizardly powers, but there are no guarantees, and unfortunately no yellow brick road. Oz may simply be a dream but the lessons learned are significant. The opportunity to make friends and gain insight along the way, make the journey worthwhile— even with the occasional Wicked Witch or flying monkeys.

References

Agre, P. (1999). Life after cyberspace. European Association for the Study of Science and Technology Review, 18, 2-5.

Barabatsis, G., Fegan, M., & Hansen, K. (1999). The performance of cyberspace: An exploration into computer-mediated reality. Journal of Computer Mediated Communication, 5.

Baym, N. K. (1998). The emergence of online community. In S. Jones (Ed.), Cybersociety 2.0 (pp. 35-68). Thousand Oaks, CA: Sage.

Deflem, M. (1991). Ritual, anti-structure and religion: A discussion of Victor Turner's processual symbolic analysis. Journal for the Scientific Study of Religion, 30, 1-25.

Hafner, K. (1997). The epic saga of the WELL. Wired, 5(5).

Hauben, M., & Hauben, R. (1999). Netizens. On the history and the impact of the net. Retrieved August 8, 2000, from http://www.columbia.edu/~hauben/netbook/

Kiesler, S., Siegel, J., & McGuire. (1984). Social-psychological aspects of computer-mediated communication. American Psychologist, 39, 1123-1134.

LeRoy, M. (Producer), & Fleming, V. (Director). (1939). The Wizard of Oz [Motion picture]. United States: Metro-Goldwyn-Mayer.

Locke, C., Levine, R., Searls, D., & Weinberger, D. (2001). The cluetrain manifesto: The end of business as usual. New York: Perseus Books Group.

Maslow, A. (1943). A theory of human motivation. Psychological Review, 50, 370-396.

Maslow, A. (1954). Motivation and Personality. New York: Harper.

Matei, S. (2001). From counterculture to cyberculture. Virtual community discourse and the dilemma of modernity. Unpublished Paper.

Miller, D. P. (2004). Searching for God knows what. Colorado Springs, CO: Nelson Books.

Preece, J. (2000). Online communities. Designing usability, supporting sociability. New York: John Wiley & Sons, Ltd.

Rheingold, H. (1993). The virtual community: Homesteading on the electronic frontier (1st ed.). New York: Harper Perennial.

VIRTUAL SOCIABILITY

Brenda Berkelaar

 Rheingold, H. (2000). The virtual community: Homesteading on the electronic frontier (Rev. ed.). Cambridge, MA: MIT Press.

Sanger, L. (2005). The early history of Nupedia and Wikipedia: A memoir [Electronic Version]. SlashDot. Retrieved from http://features.slashdot.org/article.pl?sid=05/04/18/164213&tid=95

Schiff, S. (2006, July 31). Know it all. The New Yorker.

Seabrook, J. (1997). Deeper. New York: Simon & Schuster.

Stoll, C. (1996). Silicon snake oil: Second thoughts on the information highway. New York: Anchor Books.

Toennies, F. (1988). Community and society: Gemeinschaft and gesellschaft (New ed.). New York: Transaction Publishers.

Turner, E., (2004). Rites of Communitas. In Frank A. Salamone (Ed.), Encyclopedia of religious rites, rituals, and festivals (pp. 97-101). New York: Routledge.

Turner, V. (1995). The ritual process: Structure and ant-structure. Chicago: Aldine Publishing Company.

Wahba, M. A., & Bridwell, L. G. (1976). Maslow reconsidered: A review of research on need hierarchy theory. Organizational Behavior and Human Performance, 15, 212-240.

Walther, J. B., & Parks, M. R. (2002). Cues filtered out, cues filtered in: Computer-mediated communication _ and relationships. In M. L. Knapp & J. A. Daly (Eds.), Handbook of interpersonal communication (3rd ed., pp. 529-563). Thousand Oaks, CA: Sage.

Weinberger, D. (2002). Small pieces loosely joined. Cambridge, MA: Perseus.

Wellman, B. (2001). Physical place and cyber place: The rise of personalized networks. International Journal of Urban and Regional Research, 25(2), 227-252.

Wenger, E., McDermott, R., & Snyder, W. M. (2002). Cultivating communities of practice: A guide to managing knowledge. Boston, MA: Harvard Business School Press.

Wolf, G. (2004). How the Internet invented Howard Dean [Electronic Version]. Wired, 12. Retrieved October 19, 2006 from http://www.wired.com/wired/archive/12.01/dean.html?pg=1&topic=&topic_set =

The Invisible Man: Speaking into the Online Void

Brian C. Britt

http://ubimark.com/in/books/582/

Abstract

The Internet is one of the most prominent media of the 21st century. A common assumption is that people participate in online communities in order to socialize and form relationships. However, the lack of visible personal identity creates an environment in which users seek only to be heard, not to interact. Some of the most successful social networking sites are geared toward self-expression. Those that try to emphasize socialization suffer from having an obscure audience and eventually tend toward self-expression. Future research includes the exploration of a possible inverse relationship between free speech and social support, and the relationship between lurkers and contributions.

Over the last two decades, online communities have grown exponentially in popularity. Just as 56k modems have been replaced by T1 networks, our interactions with, as Howard Rheingold (2001) described, our "family of invisible friends" (p. xv) have exploded in frequency.

This is not to say that our online activities are the same now as they were 20 years ago, of course. The days when we were excited to send an E-mail are far behind us. That thrill has long since been replaced by guild assaults on possessed dragons, demon lords, and bikini-clad warlocks in World of Warcraft.

While our activities may have evolved, however, online communities themselves persist. From visually intoxicating multiplayer role playing games to bulletin board systems reminiscent of Rheingold's classic  "Whole Earth 'Lectronic Link," or WELL (Rheingold, 2001), we can't pull ourselves away from the virtual venues. Even Facebook's bold claim of "350 million active users" (Facebook, 2010), which would make it more heavily populated than every country except for China and India (Central Intelligence Agency, 2010), is somehow unsurprising in this electronic age.

More than anything else, the Internet is a place for self-expression. According to Jeremiah Owyang, senior analyst for Forrester Research, one in every four Americans has a personal blog on MySpace (Owyang, 2008). Factor in the number of people who use similar Web sites like Twitter and Facebook – the latter of which passed MySpace as the most popular social networking site in April 2008 – and it is clear that the majority of people today actively use the Internet to express themselves.

As opposed to use of the above sites, which highlight personal status updates, our online social activities are not as clear. Consider those individuals who join online discussion groups to talk about particular topics. On the surface, this may appear to suggest that socialization is an important reason for joining an online community. What is often lost in these supposed interactions, however, is whether people are forming social bonds or merely announcing their own views back and forth as if in a debate. Furthermore, can anyone really say he or she is online to interact with others if no one ever bothers to see who is hiding behind the username?

Brian C. Britt

So our question is this: Why do people join Internet communities? Do they do so to meet other people and to form personal relationships? Or do they do it simply to be heard?

The Invisible Me

One of the first facets of Internet use that a neophyte may notice is that, whenever you do something, no one is watching. If you walk into the library to search for a book, you never know when an acquaintance could appear for a chance encounter. When you run a Web search, however, not only are your results retrieved in seconds, but your identity remains hidden behind a generic Internet Protocol (IP) address.

The same is true of most online communities compared with those in the "real world." If a person unthinkingly says something foolish to her peers, it could negatively affect their impressions of her on a long-term scale. There might be broader consequences if it involves someone in a position of authority, such as an employer. Her salary might be affected, and it could inhibit her ability to obtain a positive reference if she ever seeks employment elsewhere.

On the other hand, aggravating an authority figure online would have a comparatively minimal impact. Her salary would certainly be unaffected, and it would not make looking for a forum elsewhere any more difficult. The worst-case scenario would be for her to find a different venue and use a different username. In any case, no matter what happened in the past, she could always start over with no consequences.

This apparent immunity is an essential aspect of the Internet. Anonymity makes it a safe haven in which anyone can say anything and not face retribution later.

http://ubimark.com/in/books/582/

This is largely the cause of some communities experiencing what John Seabrook (1997) called "thrashes." A thrash, as he put it, was a "wild, raging battle" (p. 152) that might have erupted into a fistfight had it occurred  anywhere but online. But thanks to usernames and a few miles of space, even the most intense fights left few scars.

Some social media, in fact, take an extreme approach toward anonymity. The controversial image board 4chan, for instance, does not tie posters to a particular name. Users may choose to adopt a username before posting, but there is little point in doing so since anyone else can assume the same alias at any time. Therefore, members cannot develop their reputations and there are virtually no consequences for what is said.

Granted, many Web sites explicitly require users to provide their real name when registering. For instance, Facebook's terms of service demand that "You will not provide any false personal information on Facebook, or create an account for anyone other than yourself without permission," and even that "You will keep your contact information accurate and up-to-date" (Facebook, 2009). In theory, this means that users' online actions could have far-reaching effects in their personal lives, as anything said online could easily be tracked back to their physical selves. In reality, however, it is quite common for users to break the rules and set up accounts under false identities (Jesdanun, 2008). This means that, rules aside, users can still keep their activities on a given Web site separate from those offline as well as on any other site.

Does the complete absence of personal identity – which increases users' freedom to speak but weakens

Brian C. Britt

 the network between members – help or hurt activity? Considering that 4chan is "one of the Internet's most trafficked 'image boards'" (Sarno, 2008), and that it averages over 150,000 posts per day in its "random" board, or "/b/," alone (Grossman, 2008), free speech seems to be the primary concern.

In general, Internet users want to be noticed. This was reflected by Ling et al. (2005), whose study adjusted different social aspects of online communities in an attempt to increase contributions. All but two of their methods failed. Assigning more difficult goals to communities as opposed to easy tasks marginally increased activity; more importantly, however, emphasizing the uniqueness of contributions had a significant positive impact on the quantity of contributions. In other words, the more that others notice your comments, the more likely you are to talk.

People don't have to be friends with you or even know who you are. All that matters is that they recognize that you are some entity who is doing something.

Hey, Look at Me!

The idea of "social networking," heavily emphasized by Facebook and MySpace, seems to suggest that online communities foster social interactions between their members. This claim, however, deserves further scrutiny.

What is the nature of a "social network"? According to boyd and Ellison (2007), the idea has changed in the last several years. "Early public online communities such as Usenet and public discussion forums were structured by topics or according to topical hierarchies, but social network sites are structured as personal (or

'egocentric') networks, with the individual at the center of their own community" (boyd & Ellison, 2007).
Facebook, the fourth-most visited Web site in the world (Schonfeld, 2009), is an excellent example of a "social network" that pays little attention to the group. Consider one of its most unique features, the use of "applications." These are programs that individual users create which may be used in the profiles of others on Facebook.

While applications range from Scrabble clones to Easter egg hunts, let us examine the most actively used applications: "Photos," "Super Wall," "Top Friends," and "Video" (Facebook, 2008).[1] Of these four, only "Top Friends" would appear to emphasize interaction, and it is actually used simply to rank one's acquaintances: telling them what you think. The other three, "Photos," "Super Wall," and "Video," combine to transform any Facebook profile into a traditional blog with images, comments, and film.

At first glance, this might still seem to support social interaction. The idea of the "blogosphere" has been publicized as a way in which ordinary people can

---

[1] While more current data about application use is available through other sources (e.g. O'Neill, 2009), these figures are misleading because of recent changes to Facebook's Terms of Service. Several major applications whose functions were largely focused on membership accumulation alone were suspended or otherwise restricted (Arrington, 2008, July 7), which promoted the growth of competing features that Facebook itself offered to all users (such as the "Wall" and "Photos" sections). These standard features are not considered by Facebook to be "applications" and therefore feature no activity tracking, so it is impossible to objectively compare them against those which must be added voluntarily.

Brian C. Britt

 engage in discussion in the public sphere. The problem with this notion is that "diary-style personal blogs make up the heart and soul of the blogosphere" (Kornblum, 2003). Few people jump into political discourse through their blogs, but half a decade ago, hundreds of thousands had blogs ranging "from teen journals filled with angst to young professionals musing about their jobs and lives" (Kornblum, 2003). As electronic diaries, blogs offer minimal interaction, and Facebook doesn't go far beyond that level.

Facebook and its users have certainly tried to create a community using applications. For instance, the leading instant messaging application "Chat!" has over 317,000 monthly active users. That sounds like a lot until you compare it with "iLike," the 18th-most used application on Facebook, with almost 10 million monthly active users (O'Neill, 2009). By this measure, it would seem that telling people what songs you like is over thirty times more important than actually talking with them. In fact, each of the top ten applications has over 15 million users. The unimportant "Chat!" ranks at #266 (O'Neill, 2009).[2]

The observed lack of socialization also holds true when looking at the quantity of applications rather than the leaders. Yau (2008) of FlowingData analyzed all 23,160 Facebook applications and found that a large majority of almost 10,000 were purely "just for fun,"

---

[2] While "Chat!" suffers from competition with Facebook's standard chat feature, "iLike" similarly competes with Facebook-supported fan groups for movies, music, and more. Because both functions compete against Facebook itself, the comparison between the two is still valid and the disparity remains noteworthy.

http://ubimark.com/in/books/582/

while their "messaging" counterparts failed to reach 2,000.

If that wasn't enough, consider the biggest difference between Facebook and traditional communitas: the lack of interaction with other users. Yes, it's possible to communicate with your friends, but everyone beyond that is nothing more than a name and a shrunken avatar. With the exception of those who hack the system, users are unable to even view most profiles aside from those of their friends.

The natural consequence of this is that it is difficult to connect with anyone outside of one's pre-existing social circle. While early communitas like the WELL encouraged free interaction, today's biggest social network has instead artfully restricted it. What results, then, is not a massive community of 350 million members but a collection of small, egocentric groups composed of people who the central user already knew before joining.

Why visit Facebook at all, then? There are two main reasons. The first is simple: fun. With nearly innumerable user-created applications, it's hard for many to stay away. After all, who doesn't like using the popular "SuperPoke" to throw flaming bags of poop at others (Facebook, 2008)?

This example also satisfies the second purpose of Facebook use: the illusion of attention. It's nice to think that other people care about what you say online. That's the whole purpose of a blog, after all. While "Chat!" does little to turn Facebook into a community, "SuperPoke" gives any user a chance to yell, "Hey everyone, look at what I just did!" (Facebook, 2008)

Facebook is all about the individual user, not about interacting with others. Aside from "Super Wall," which

Brian C. Britt

 lets readers post responses to a user and his or her comments – very much like the oft-overlooked "guestbook" on many blogs – most of the top applications offer no opportunity for even shallow feedback. In the end, Facebook is just an opportunity to stand on a pedestal and preach.

The Invisible Audience

Web sites that actually try to create communities are another matter entirely. The WELL's framework and mission are far from outdated; countless bulletin board systems, Wikis, and other variants now walk along the trail it helped to blaze. Doesn't that mean, then, that many Internet users come online for the social aspect? Could it be that they strive to be part of a community?

Since many modern online communities closely resemble the WELL, let us look back to its beginning in order to better understand present systems. The WELL, which started as an extension of the Whole Earth Catalog, was primarily composed of intelligent, middle-aged baby boomers looking for a club. Larry Brilliant first proposed the idea of an online community to Stewart Brand in 1984. Past failures had taught Brilliant that a certain collection of people was necessary to make his idea come to life, and he "thought he could find that ready-made user community around Stewart Brand" (Hafner, 1997).

This is exactly the problem. The WELL's origins were a group of people who were already connected. People didn't find the WELL through a search engine; they heard of it through their friends, who had in turn learned of it through their friends.

http://ubimark.com/in/books/582/

In fact, many of the most memorable interactions between "WELLites" occurred offline, at organized functions hosted by moderators. As Rheingold said, "The WELL felt like an authentic community to me from the start  because it was grounded in my everyday physical world.... By now, I've attended real-life WELL marriages, WELL births, and even a WELL funeral" (Rheingold, 2001, p. xvi).

As such, the WELL wasn't a community of its own accord. It merely offered another venue in which people who were already connected could communicate, much like Facebook users are only able to connect with their offline friends.

What of social networks that aren't tied to the physical world? Do people visit those sites in order to socialize?

Kiesler, Siegel & McGuire (1984) offered evidence to the contrary. As they noted, "Communicators must imagine their audience, for at a terminal it almost seems as if the computer itself is the audience" (p. 1125). Kraut et al. (1998) later reported that Internet use actually caused loneliness and isolation rather than enhancing personal connections. Once again, the audience is a faceless entity – the diary is no different than ever, even if it uses circuits.

In a further exploration of this topic, Walther and Parks (2002) assessed the "cues filtered out" model proposed by Culnan and Markus (1987). In doing so, they recognized that the Internet, a "lean medium," was not the best choice for social interaction, a necessarily complex phenomenon (Walther & Parks, 2002, p. 533). Further, the main reason that a medium would be used for any purpose for which it was ill-suited was if other options failed. "Even if a [face-to-face] meeting would

Brian C. Britt

 be most efficient, such meetings cannot always be held on the spur of the moment; we walk down the hall to pay someone a visit but find the office empty, and telephone calls go unanswered, leaving e-mail, perhaps the last choice, as the first among unequals" (p. 533).

This drives to the crux of why people join online communities for self-expression rather than socialization. There are many ways to socialize. Perhaps the most relevant in this case is to join a face-to-face group and interact with those people, or to interact more within an organization with whom one is already affiliated. This is, as Walther and Parks might suggest, a more efficient and therefore more likely method of fulfilling that need.

Self-expression, on the other hand, is much different. If a person writes his thoughts in a journal, no one else will read it. Sending letters would help him reach a few people, but not many. Phone calls would have similarly ineffective results. A letter to the editor of the local newspaper might result in a few hundred or thousand people seeing the message – assuming it gets published, which may be unlikely. And the average person can forget about expensive mass media like TV, which would otherwise be an ideal option for self-expression.

The Internet, however, is open for all to use. Anyone sitting at a computer can join a group and start talking immediately. There's no need to even buy Web space: the platform on which users speak has already been purchased on their behalf. Better yet, anyone in the world may, at some point, see their messages. It's a cost-effective, easy-to-access medium with theoretically unlimited viewership.

All other options for speaking to the masses have serious detriments. The Internet stands out as the best option – for self-expression, not for socialization.

Critiques and Future Research

Several authors have rallied behind the idea of online socialization. This is unsurprising, as Rheingold (2000) described his own experiences with the WELL and its members as "realer than we had bargained for" (p. 325). Since the WELL was so heavily based in offline interactions, its realness makes perfect sense.

Others such as Wellman (2001) arbitrarily defined online communities as serving a social need, citing qualities such as "The ability to connect with multiple social milieus, with limited involvement in each milieu," "Increased choices in milieus in which to get involved," and "The decreased commitment of each milieu to its inhabitants' well-being" as important social points. In fact, the first two statements strongly support the notion that the Internet can best be used for self-expression – you can speak anywhere about anything – while the latter shows that online social support is minimal.

Ridings and Gefen (2004) attempted to pose another significant counterpoint, listing friendship as the second-most important reason for joining an online group behind information exchange. Their research is problematic, however, because they did not measure the importance of self-expression in relation to the other variables. Some of their noted respondents, in fact, appeared to indicate such a desire:

- "I like talking about baseball"

Brian C. Britt

- "I can easily let out my emotions here and others will understand."
- "also because some times its easier to write things down than to say them" (Ridings & Gefen, 2004)

These self-centered responses need to be explored beyond their initial categorizations; otherwise, we cannot adequately compare the relative importance of socialization and free speech based on the qualitative assessment.

The ability to speak freely may, in fact, be inversely correlated with the level of social support. Consider the case of Megan Meier, who committed suicide after being ostracized on MySpace (ABC News, 2007). Lori Drew, who allegedly drove Meier to suicide, was only brought to charges because she purportedly registered on MySpace under a fake name (Jesdanun, 2008). She was later convicted of computer fraud for violating MySpace's user agreement (Steinhauer, 2008); while the jury reduced the charges from felonies to misdemeanors, the decision nonetheless set a precedent that would make hiding one's identity while online illegal in countless venues. The effects of this decision on user behavior, and in turn the effects of such possible new behaviors on users' perceptions of socialization and community, have yet to be conclusively studied.

Another useful avenue for research would be the role of lurkers. Those who view a community but contribute nothing to it clearly violate the principle of joining a group in order to be heard. Are lurkers true members of a community? What motivates them to transition from lengthy silence to active contributions? Are they trying to acclimate themselves to their environment before jumping on their metaphorical soapboxes, or does

lurking satisfy some sort of voyeuristic need? How does the presence and magnitude of lurkers impact the desire for others to contribute to a particular venue? Are lurkers more or less important to posters than their fellow contributors?

Motivating people to contribute to online communities is a difficult process. By analyzing the effects that regulations and viewers have, these groups can better cater to their members' need to speak rather than attempting to force socialization upon them.

References

ABC News. (November 19, 2007). Parents: Cyber bullying led to teen's suicide. Retrieved from http://abcnews.go.com/GMA/Story?id=3882520

Arrington, M. (2008, June 12). Facebook No Longer The Second Largest Social Network. Message posted to http://www.techcrunch.com/2008/06/12/facebook-no-longer-the-second-largest-social-network/

Arrington, M. (2008, July 7). Facebook Continues War On App Developers. This Week: Super Wall. Message posted to http://www.techcrunch.com/2008/07/07/facebook-continues-war-on-app-developers-this-week-super-wall/

Bosskillers. (2008). Retrieved October 21, 2008, from http://www.bosskillers.com/

boyd, d. m., & Ellison, N. B. (2007). Social network sites: Definition, history, and scholarship. *Journal of Computer-Mediated Communication, 13*(1), article 11.

VIRTUAL SOCIABILITY

Brian C. Britt

 Central Intelligence Agency. (2010). The World Factbook -- Country Comparison :: Population. Retrieved January 21, 2009, from https://www.cia.gov/library/publications/the-world-factbook/rankorder/2119rank.html

Culnan, M. J., & Markus, M. L. (1987). Information technologies. In F. M. Jablin, L. L. Putnam, K. H. Roberts, & L. W. Porter (Eds.), *Handbook of organizational communication: An interdisciplinary perspective* (pp. 420-443). Newbury Park, CA: Sage.

EUROPA. (2009). European Countries. Retrieved August 19, 2009, from http://europa.eu/abc/european_countries/index_en.htm

Facebook. (2008). Application Directory. Retrieved October 20, 2008, from http://www.facebook.com/apps/

Facebook. (2009). Statement of Rights and Responsibilities. Retrieved August 18, 2009, from http://www.facebook.com/terms.php

Facebook. (2010). Statistics. Retrieved January 21, 2010, from http://www.facebook.com/press/info.php?statistics

Grossman, L. (2008, July 10). Now in Paper-Vision: The 4chan Guy. Message posted to http://time-blog.com/nerd_world/2008/07/now_in_papervision_the_4chan_g.html

Hafner, K. (1997). The epic saga of the Well. *Wired, 5*(5).

Jesdanun, A. (2008, May 18). Routine conduct at risk after MySpace case. *USA Today.* Retrieved from http://www.usatoday.com/news/nati on/2008-05-18-internet-suicide-legal_N.htm

Kiesler, S., Siegel, J., & McGuire. (1984). Social psychological aspects of computer mediated communication. *American Psychologist, 39*(10), 1123-1134.

The Invisible Man

http://ubimark.com/in/books/582/

Kornblum, J. (2003, July 8). Welcome to the Blogosphere. *USA Today*. Retrieved October 20, 2008, from https://web.ics.purdue.edu/~smatei/435/readings/welcomeblogosphere.htm

Kraut, R., Lundmark, V., Patterson, M., Kiesler, S., Mukopadhyay, T., & Scherlis, W. (1998). Internet paradox: A social technology that reduces social involvement and psychological well-being? *American Psychologist, 53*, 1017-1031.

Ling, K., Beenen, G., Ludford, P., Wang, X., Chang, K., Li, X., . . . Kraut, R. (2005). Using social psychology to motivate contributions to online communities. *Journal of Computer-Mediated Communication, 10*(4), article 10.

O'Neill, N. (2009). Facebook Application Leaderboard. *All Facebook*. Retrieved August 18, 2009, from http://statistics.allfacebook.com/applications/leaderboard/-/-/m/DESC/-/

Owyang, J. (2008, January 9). Social Network Stats: Facebook, MySpace, Reunion (Jan, 2008). Message posted to http://www.web-strategist.com/blog/2008/01/09/social-network-stats-facebook-myspace-reunion-jan-2008/

Owyang, J. (2009, January 11). A Collection of Social Network Stats for 2009. Message posted to http://www.web-strategist.com/blog/2009/01/11/a-collection-of-soical-network-stats-for-2009/

Rheingold, H. (2000). *The Virtual Community: homesteading on the electronic frontier* (Rev. ed.). Cambridge, MA: MIT Press.

Rheingold, H. (2001). *The Virtual Community: homesteading on the electronic frontier* (1st HarperPerennial ed.). New York, NY: HarperPerennial.

 Ridings, C., & Gefen, D. (2004). Virtual Community Attraction: Why People Hang Out Online. *Journal of Computer-Mediated Communication, 10*(1), article 4.

Sarno, D. (2008, July 12). Rise and fall of the Googled swastika. *Los Angeles Times.* Retrieved from http://articles.latimes.com/2008/jul/12/entertainment/et-swastika12

Schonfeld, E. (2009, August 4). Facebook Is Now the Fourth-Largest Site In The World. Retrieved from http://www.techcrunch.com/2009/08/04/facebook-is-now-the-fourth-largest-site-in-the-world/

Seabrook, J. (1997). *Deeper.* New York, NY: Simon & Schuster.

Steinhauer, J. (2008, November 26). Verdict in MySpace Suicide Case. *The New York Times*, p. A25.

Walther, J. B., & Parks, M. R. (2002). Cues filtered out, cues filtered in: Computer-mediated communication and relationships. In M. L. Knapp & J. A. Daly (Eds.), *Handbook of interpersonal communication* (3rd ed., pp. 529-563). Thousand Oaks, CA: Sage.

Wellman, B. (2001). Physical place and cyber place: the rise of personalized networks. *International Journal of Urban and Regional Research, 25*(2), 227-252.

Yau, N. (2008, May 1). Chart of the Day: A Breakdown of Facebook Applications. Message posted to http://flowingdata.com/2008/05/01/chart-of-the-day-a-breakdown-of-facebook-applications/

Welcome to I-berspace: Media Gratifications in Successful Virtual Communities

Robert N. Yale

http://ubimark.com/in/books/583/

Abstract

This essay posits that virtual communities are successful to the degree that participants fulfill multiple gratifications within the medium. The greater the number of participants fulfilling multiple gratifications within the group space, the more community-like the group becomes. This sliding-scale conception of virtual community allows groups to be ranked in terms of their community-likeness, and may explain why some groups fail to be become vibrant virtual communities. This essay examines the historical example of the WELL (Whole Earth 'Lectronic Link) as an exemplar virtual community that provided multiple gratifications for many of its users and continues with an analysis of the blogosphere and Wikipedia as modern virtual communities with differing degrees of success.

Ask any parent of a toddler, and they will most likely tell you that selfishness is not a virtue. Incessant cries of "that's *mine!*" and "*I* want..." are often among the first utterances of children, signaling a nearly innate human selfishness. As time goes by, most children are socially conditioned to consider not only their individual needs, but also the needs of others around them. In the arena of online interaction, I believe that virtual communities thrive when a critical mass of members begin to use the community space to meet their own individual needs. This is not to say that interaction in these virtual

Robert Yale

communities is devoid of the consideration of others, but that even altruistic actions have underlying selfish motives. Rheingold (2000) provides a glimpse into this dichotomy in one explanation of why he found the WELL (Whole Earth 'Lectronic Link) so compelling: "I find that the help I receive far outweighs the energy I expend helping others: a marriage of altruism and self-interest" (p. 47). It is a reconceptualization of cyberspace, a virtual "place" created by the connection of many networks to the Internet, as I-berspace, a virtual place where individuals seek and obtain individual gratifications, which provides the necessary framework for judging the relative success of virtual communities. When a critical mass of users routinely seeks and obtains gratifications within the group space, virtual community is born.

Uses and Gratifications Theory (Katz, Blumler, & Gurevitch, 1974) provides a framework for understanding why people choose specific media. It postulates that people actively seek out specific media and specific content in order to generate specific gratifications. In this way, media competes for the attention of individuals. Within the framework of this theory, it follows that a virtual community (medium) that is actively sought to fulfill multiple gratifications will be more successful (community-like) than a virtual community where fewer gratifications are sought and obtained.

This essay posits that virtual communities are successful to the degree that participants obtain multiple gratifications within the medium. The greater the number of participants fulfilling multiple gratifications within the group space, the more community-like the group becomes. In order to make this contention clear, a few definitions are in order.  Within this essay, virtual community is defined as any group of individuals who interact with one another on a regular basis via computer mediated communication. This definition is bound to be unsatisfying to many, but within the framework of this essay, it is particularly appropriate because it allows the concept of virtual community to exist as a scale where the level of community-likeness can be measured, rather than as a binary, where different interpretations of community deem specific virtual groups as "true" or "false" virtual communities. The concept of gratifications in this essay comes from McQuail's (1983) typology of gratifications sought and obtained from the media. This typology is more understandable than the original gratification categories specified by Katz, Blumler, and Gurevitch (1974), and is more suited for this analysis. Table 1 presents gratification categories and relevant examples identified by McQuail. The gratification categories identified in this table will be referred to numerous times in the essay as relevant examples from virtual communities are identified.

Group space is a particularly important term in this analysis because it differentiates communication between individual group members and communication between an individual and the group. The group space is identified by its accessibility to all group members – thus, communication posted to a common area such as an open forum occurs in the group space while communication sent via private message (e.g., e-mail) to another individual or sub-group is not.

Robert Yale

Table 1: Typology of Gratifications
Sought and Obtained from the Media[1]

Gratification Category	Examples
Information	<ul><li>Finding out about relevant events and conditions in immediate surroundings, society, and the world</li><li>Seeking advice on practical matters, or opinion and decision choices</li><li>Satisfying curiosity and general interest</li><li>Learning, self-education</li><li>Gaining a sense of security through knowledge</li></ul>
Personal Identity	<ul><li>Finding reinforcement for personal values</li><li>Finding models of behavior</li><li>Identifying with valued others (in the media)</li><li>Gaining insight into one's self</li></ul>
Integration and Social Interaction	<ul><li>Gaining insight into circumstances of others: social empathy</li><li>Identifying with others and gaining a new sense of belonging</li><li>Finding a basis for conversation and social interaction</li><li>Having a substitute for real-life</li></ul>

---

[1] McQuail, 1983, pp. 82-83

http://ubimark.com/in/books/583/

	companionship
	▪ Helping to carry out social roles
	▪ Enabling one to connect with family, friends, and society
Entertainment	▪ Escaping, or being diverted from, problems
	▪ Relaxing
	▪ Getting intrinsic cultural or aesthetic enjoyment
	▪ Filling time
	▪ Emotional Release
	▪ Sexual Arousal

In order to advance the argument that virtual communities are successful to the degree that participants fulfill multiple gratifications within the group space, I will examine relevant literature surrounding the communities of the WELL, the blogosphere, and Wikipedia.

Gratifications on the WELL

Any examination of virtual community would be incomplete without mention of the Whole Earth 'Lectronic Link (WELL), one of the best known early examples of virtual community. The WELL began in 1985 as an experiment launched by Larry Brilliant and Stewart Brand, designed to "take a group of interesting people, give them the means to stay in continuous communication with one another, stand back, and see what happens" (Hafner, 1997, para. 16). Brand, the

Robert Yale

 publisher of the Whole Earth Review, used the print magazine to advertise the nascent online forum, and word of mouth slowly caused the user base of the WELL to grow. During the summer of 1985, one of the WELL's most famous members and ardent supporters logged on for the first time and joined the discussion. Howard Rheingold, or "hlr," as he was identified on the WELL forums, provides a cheery glimpse of life on the WELL in his 1993 book, *The Virtual Community: Homesteading on the Electronic Frontier.* In contrast, John Seabrook, a columnist for the New Yorker, has written a less enthusiastic report about WELL interaction in his 1997 book, *Deeper: My Two-Year Odyssey in Cyberspace.* These texts provide interesting insight into the varying perceptions of the WELL as a virtual community. One author (Rheingold) wholeheartedly jumps into the medium and almost immediately begins fulfilling each of the gratifications identified by McQuail, while the other (Seabrook) is more tentative in his adoption of the medium for gratification, and seems to find noticeably less "community" within the same environment.

Rheingold is not shy about his immediate fascination with and attachment to the WELL. The opening paragraph of the book relates his amazement that he was able to find out how to remove a tick from his daughter's head via a post on the WELL faster than his wife was able to contact a pediatrician. He recalls being amazed at "the speed with which we obtained precisely the information we needed to know, right when we needed to know it," and related feeling an "immense inner sense of security that comes with discovering that real people [...] are available, around the clock, if you need them" (Rheingold, 2000, p. 1). Seabrook similarly

http://ubimark.com/in/books/583/

experienced awe at the ability of the community to provide information about seemingly limitless topics, and used the term "groupmind" to refer to the vast collective knowledge and experience held by the WELL  community. He notes "the groupmind's breadth of knowledge consistently amazed me. On several occasions, having posted in the Books Conference a request for obscure information about an author, or in the Grateful Dead conference about a version of a song, I received a correct, informed answer back within two hours" (Seabrook, 1997, p. 199). These anecdotes clearly demonstrate the use of the virtual community to gratify a need for information, with Rheingold "seeking advice on practical matters" and "gaining a sense of security through knowledge," and Seabrook "satisfying curiosity and general interest" while engaging in "learning [and] self-education" as identified by McQuail (1983, p. 82).

Rheingold found the WELL to be a compelling environment to gratify the need for personal identity. He notes that in a traditional community, one is limited to those who are geographically close to find "people who share our values," while in a virtual community, there are no geographic restrictions, and one can "go directly to the place where our favorite subjects are being discussed, then get acquainted with people who share our passions or use words in a way we find attractive" (Rheingold, 2000, p. 11). He tells the story of Blair Newman, a larger-than-life persona on the WELL, a former cocaine addict who seemed to transfer his addiction to the WELL, but who found the expression on the WELL to be cathartic and self-revealing. "Blair called it Compconf Psychserv. It was cheaper than drugs,

Robert Yale

 cheaper than shrinks, and it kept him off the street" (p. 19).

By Rheingold's (2000) account, perhaps the gratification that the WELL was most successful at fulfilling was in the category of integration and social interaction. One of the conferences he speaks most fondly about in his book is the Parenting conference, full of devoted parents trading tips and insights to help them carry out their social roles as parents. Rheingold relates the emotional story of WELL user Philcat's son, Gabe, who was diagnosed with leukemia. After posting this information in the Parenting conference, floods of well-wishers indicated their emotional support and empathy for the family. During the following weeks, members of the conference learned about blood disorders, the blood donation system, and how to advocate for children in hospitals. In the parenting conference, users "began to realize [...] that we had the power not only to use words to share feelings and exchange helpful information, but to accomplish things in the real world" (p. 12).

Rheingold's use of the WELL "for an average of two hours a day, seven days a week," and his excitement at discovering "writing as a performing art" indicate the use of the WELL to gratify the need for entertainment. Rheingold, far from seeing his responsibilities as a host on the WELL as tedious, found intrinsic enjoyment in the online activity. Seabrook, on the other hand, didn't ever really connect with other individuals via the WELL. Instead, he existed primarily as a "lurker," a user who spent time on the system reading posts and keeping up with events in the conferences, but who rarely submitted in his own posts. A particularly interesting incident occurred when Seabrook wrote a story about the WELL in the New Yorker which was not received kindly by the other users. The [media] The New Yorker conference was buzzing with talk of the article when users discovered that Seabrook himself had been watching  the conversation. One user engaged Seabrook with a direct question about the content of his article, and he was forced to join the conversation himself, an altogether unpleasant experience (Seabrook, 1997). Seabrook seemed to prefer to use the WELL to gratify the need for information and entertainment, while eschewing the forum to seek personal identity or integration and social interaction.

Overall, Seabrook's (1997) picture of the WELL as a virtual community is darker and less optimistic than Rheingold's. Far from Rheingold's (2000) utopian "third place" where "people can rebuild the aspects of community that were lost when the malt shop became a mall" (p. 10), Seabrook (1997) found it "useless [...] to think of the WELL as any kind of utopia. It was like anywhere else, a place where there was authority to be grabbed, and where I would naturally figure out a way to grab it if I wanted to, just like I had in boarding school" (p. 213). There are an infinite number of possible explanations about why Seabrook and Rheingold came to such differing views of the same online group. I contend that Seabrook's melancholy outlook is a direct result of his reticence to seek the gratifications of personal identity and social integration. Thus, for Seabrook, the WELL fell short of being a compelling virtual community, not because of any intrinsic lack, but because as a journalist with a goal of objectivity, he failed to wholly experience it.

Robert Yale

Gratifications in the Blogosphere

Blogging, as a means of communicating information, has gone from the eccentric activity of a few to the latest wave in corporate marketing. Film studios, soft drink makers, auto manufacturers, and software developers are among the companies now using blogs as a way to connect with customers (Anderson, 2004). The meteoric rise in popularity of blogs over the past five years has caused some to examine the phenomena as a possible environment for virtual communities, each blog or blog-ring potentially hosting its own mini virtual community. In keeping with the previously defined concept of virtual community, only blogs with a "group space" may be considered candidate for community. Within the architecture of most blogs, this group space takes the form of comment pages, where blog readers can respond to the blog author(s) and to each other's comments. Some blogs allow interested users to sign up and become contributors, or to host their own blog within the framework of the larger system, posting their own topics and receiving feedback from readers and fellow bloggers. Daily Kos and Free Republic are two notable examples of political blogs that allow an unlimited number of contributors, and whose contributors interact with one another via the framework of the blogging host. In is in this space that virtual community may blossom.

Information is clearly a gratification that many blogs directly attempt to provide for their readers. Salam Pax, a 29 year old blogger in Baghdad, Iraq, found his blog "postings on the mood of the city as it awaited the U.S. invasion riveted readers around the world." Glenn Reynolds, host of the political news and opinion blog

Instapundit, highlights the idea that blogs provide a resource for those seeking the opinions of others. He states: "Blogs are reproducing something people thought for a long time we had lost, the discussion in the  public sphere by the ordinary people" (Kornblum, 2003). Dan Gillmor, in the preface to his book *We the Media*, tells the story of blogging during a speech by then Qwest CEO Joe Nacchio. After receiving a tip from a blog reader informing him of some opportunistic financial moves made by Nacchio as his company began to falter, Gillmor immediately posted a link to the incriminating information on his blog, and noticed an almost immediate "chill" in the audience toward the speaker – no doubt influenced by the new information exposed on the live blog (Gillmor, 2004).

Many blogs also provide an opportunity for gratification in the category of personal identity, although this is probably much more the case for the blogger than the commenting members of the virtual community. The "diary-style personal blogs [which] make up the heart and soul of the blogosphere" are unquestionably used by many authors as reflexive spaces to write about personal events, feelings, and relationships. Blogs dedicated to celebrity photos, sightings, and gossip provide readers and writers alike with the ability to "identify with valued others (in the media)" suggested by McQuail, and the topic centricity of many blogs provide an environment ripe for "finding reinforcement of personal values" (McQuail, 1983, p. 83).

Integration and social interaction is a gratification category in which most blogs either excel or ignore. Idea-centric blogs, such as the technology blog

Robert Yale

 Engadget, and cultural curiosities blog Boing Boing, don't really try to engage their readers in integration and social interaction. This type of blog use is much more common on the more personal people-centric blogs found on hosting sites like Xanga. Here, bloggers are much more likely to use their forum to talk about friends, relationships, and to link to the blogs of other people they know, providing "a basis for conversation and social interaction" and "identifying with others" (McQuail, 1983).

In the category of entertainment, blogs again provide users with the potential for gratification. Bloggers themselves might use the written word and the invisible audience as a kind of electronic escapism, or may find the writing to be therapeutic and relaxing, helping to relieve stress and provide an emotional outlet for expression. Similarly, blog readers may spend time reading blogs as a way of relaxing, filling time, or obtaining cultural or aesthetic enjoyment. With the censor-free nature of the Internet, many blogs are devoted to topics of an adult nature, allowing some readers to use blogs for the purpose of sexual arousal.

Overall, the blogging platform and the overwhelming number of idea-centric and people-centric blogs clearly provide the ability for users to engage in media gratifications in each of the categories suggested by McQuail, and any blog with a group space meets the technical requirements to host a virtual community. However, the reason so many blogs exist and so few (if any) are perceived to play host to vibrant communities may be found in the inability of a single blog to provide all four categories of media gratification for users. For example, Engadget, currently the most popular blog on

the Web according to blog search engine Technorati, does an excellent job providing readers with information and entertainment, but hardly any accommodation is made to connect users, allow them to build a sense of personal identity, and engage in social interaction. On the other hand, any random blog hosted by Xanga is likely to be filled with content intended to gratify the need for personal identity and social interaction, but is likely to be lacking in the information and entertainment categories. The general inability of most blogs to provide a space for users to obtain gratification in all four categories signals a future in which blogs as they currently exist will never achieve widespread recognition as sites for vibrant virtual communities.

Gratifications in the Wikiverse

It's doubtful that any site has received more criticism from academia or as many top 10 Google rankings as Wikipedia. "The free encyclopedia that anyone can edit" was an offshoot of the Nupedia project conceived by Jimmy Wales. The Nupedia project relied on academics and experts in their respective fields who were "to propose and write articles on subjects about which they had some knowledge." Eighteen months into the development of the Nupedia project, only 20 articles had been completed, due to a clunky "seven-stage process of editing, fact-checking, and peer review" (Sanger, 2005). Editor in chief Larry Sanger suggested to Wales that an emerging collaborative platform, called wiki, should be used to build a wiki-based encyclopedia. The new platform allows anyone with basic text tagging skills to create and edit pages on the Web site. Now, nearly seven years after the initial launch of the wiki-

 fied encyclopedia, Wikipedia has over 2 million English language articles, and more than 3 million non-English language articles.

Along with the vast amount of codified information contained within the Wikipedia domain, a vast hierarchical network of anonymous contributors, registered users, administrators, bureaucrats, stewards, and developers works to ensure the smooth operation of the encyclopedia. Wales, at the top of the hierarchy, has ultimate control over the content on the site (Pink, 2005). With such an extensive network of users collaborating via computer mediated communication to generate and format content, protect pages from electronic vandalism, and ensure the quality of the information on the site, the Wikipedia framework deserves consideration as a site for virtual community.

The ability of Wikipedia to provide information gratification for its users is undeniable. Indeed, many of the members of the Wikipedia community visited the site to find information, and stayed on as contributors. Danny Wool was engaged in an argument about Kryptonite, and in an effort to settle the debate, found himself on the Wikipedia entry. As he stumbled around the site, he noticed that each page "contained a mysterious hyperlink that said Edit" (Pink, 2005). Intrigued, Wool continued to visit the site, and a few days later made his first edit to an entry on Jewish holidays. As of March, 2005, Wool had made more Wikipedia edits than all but three contributors, over 40,000 total revisions (Pink, 2005).

In a sardonic examination of Wikipedia, Lore Sjöberg (2006) provides the following counsel for those who might wish to contribute to Wikipedia: "It will help to familiarize yourself with some of the  common terms used on Wikipedia: *meat puppet:* A person who disagrees with you. *non-notable:* A subject you're not interested in. *vandalism:* An edit you didn't make. *Neutral point of view:* your point of view." Although humorous, this excerpt provides insight into the ways that many contributors (or Wikipedians, as they are often referred) find personal identity gratification within the framework of the wiki. One author even went so far as to implicate egotism as a driving force for the average Wikipedia contributor, attributing motivation to "a dash of altruism, a dose of obsessive compulsiveness, and a good chunk of egotism" (Goetz, 2003). In arguments about entries, the contributors take sides, find those who reinforce their personal values and beliefs, and find models of behavior – all behaviors characteristic of the personal identity gratification category (McQuail, 1983).

Wikipedia's role as a site for integration and social interaction is also undeniable. According to Jimmy Wales, the users are "compulsively social, conversing with each other not only on the talk pages attached to each entry but on Wikipedia-dedicated I.R.C. channels and on user pages" (Schiff, 2006). As of July, 2006, there were over 200,000 registered users on the English-language Wikipedia site, with about 3,300 responsible for 70% of the work. These workers, in order to accomplish such a massive amount of work, necessarily engage in social interaction while they work, build friendships, and gain a sense of belonging in the Wikiverse.

It is also clear that many Wikipedians find their experiences on the site gratify a need for entertainment, using their time on the site for relaxation, filling time,

 and finding intrinsic enjoyment in the activity of creating and editing articles. Robert McHenry (2004), former editor of Encyclopædia Britannica, even conceded that "this exercise in encyclopedia making is enjoyed and even believed in fervently by many thousands of participants."

Clearly, Wikipedia provides many in its community with gratifications in all four of McQuail's categories, and as such, may be considered a successful online community. Without judgment or evaluation about the work in which the community engages, the 4000 or so volunteers who compose the core of the Wikipedia universe truly do exist in a vibrant community.

Conclusions

This essay has attempted to provide support for the contention that virtual communities are successful to the degree that participants fulfill multiple gratifications within the medium. The WELL demonstrated a virtual community where members who wholeheartedly embraced the medium and sought all four gratifications, like Howard Rheingold, found the community to be vibrant and successful. Others, like John Seabrook, failed to seek gratifications in each category, and found the WELL's promise of community to be lacking. In the blogosphere, the general inability of a single blog or blog-ring to provide users with the four gratification categories limits the medium's potential as a site for virtual community. Finally, in a modern example of vibrant community, the universe of Wikipedia provides faithful contributors with a platform through which they may seek gratification in all four categories. Future investigations of community might benefit from

Welcome to I-berspace

http://ubimark.com/in/books/583/

considering the gratifications sought and obtained by community members as a possible yard-stick by which community success may be measured.

References

Anderson, D. (2004, November). Blogs: Fad or Marketing Medium of the Future? Adweek Magazines' Technology Marketing. Retrieved October 4, 2007, from EBSCOhost.

Gillmor, D. (2004). We the Media: Grassroots Journalism by the People, for the People. New York: O'Reilly. Retrieved October 4, 2007, from http://www.authorama.com/we-the-media-1.html

Hafner, K. (1997). The Epic Saga of the Well. Wired, 5(5). Retrieved October 4, 2007, from http://www.wired.com/wired/archive/5.05/ff_well_pr.html

Katz, E., Blumler, J. G., & Gurevitch, M. (1974). Utilization of mass communication by the individual. In J. G. Blumler & E. Katz (Eds.), The Uses of Mass Communications: Current Perspectives on Gratifications Research. London: Sage.

Kornblum, J. (2003, July 8). Welcome to the Blogosphere. USA Today, p. 07d. Retrieved October 4, 2007, from EBSCOhost.

McHenry, R. (2004, November 15). The Faith-Based Encyclopedia. Retrieved October 15, 2007, from http://www.tcsdaily.com/printArticle.aspx?ID=111504A

McQuail, D. (1983). Mass Communication Theory (1st ed.). London: Sage.

Pink, D. H. (2005, March). The Book Stops Here. Wired, 1303. Retrieved October 15, 2007, from http://www.wired.com/wired/archive/13.03/wiki_pr.html

VIRTUAL SOCIABILITY

Robert Yale

 Rheingold, H. L. (2000). Virtual community: Homesteading on the electronic frontier. Cambridge, MA: MIT Press.

Sanger, L. (2005, April 18). The Early History of Nupedia and Wikipedia: A Memoir. Retrieved October 15, 2007, from http://features.slashdot.org/article.pl?sid=05/04/18/164213

Seabrook, J. (1997). Deeper: Adventures on the net. New York: Simon & Schuster.

Schiff, S. (2006, July 31). Know it All. The New Yorker. Retrieved October 15, 2007, from http://www.newyorker.com/archive/2006/07/31/060731fa_fact

Sjöberg, L. (2006, April 19). The Wikipedia FAQK. Retrieved October 4, 2007, from http://www.wired.com/software/webservices/commentary/alttext/2006/04/7067 0

Individualism Online:
Virtually Escaping the 'Massness' or Vanishing into the 'Electrovoid'?

Christina Kalinowski

http://ubimark.com/in/books/584/

Abstract
Individualism is highly valued in American culture, and its growing importance to American identity has captured researchers' attention. Not only has our cultural preoccupation with ourselves been receiving much attention, but increasingly so in conjunction with discussions of the Internet. The Internet, by its very nature, not only facilitates the expression of individualism, it has increasingly been shaped by individuals for this purpose. The Internet has been idealized by many as a utopian medium, one in which the self can be freely expressed and everyone's voice can be heard. While the Internet may provide individuals with more opportunities to express individualism, tensions exist. The expression of individualism is a solitary activity, and many sites for said expression are populated by other users; thus, there is a tension between the desire to express oneself and socially constructed norms regarding respect for others.

"Individualism lies at the very core of American culture.... We believe in the dignity, indeed the sacredness, of the individual. Anything that would violate our right to think for ourselves, judge for ourselves, make our own decisions, live our lives as we

Christina Kalinowski

 see fit, is not only morally wrong, it is sacrilegious" (Bellah et al., 2008, p. 142).

If you ask the average American to provide a list of descriptors that characterize American culture, individualism is bound to appear. Many scholars have found that not only is individualism an integral cultural component, it is also a salient identity characteristic valued by most Americans. While the cultural importance of individualism can be traced back to the roots of American history, at no previous point in time than the present has so much attention been focused on individualism and its influences upon ourselves, our social interactions, and our society. As the importance of individualism has grown, so has the many and diverse meanings that have been attributed to it; for my purposes, individualism is broadly conceptualized as expressions of self that are unique, and serve to differentiate ourselves from others. Many scholars have written of the paradoxical condition we currently find ourselves living in as a result of increasing rationalization (Bellah et al., 2008; Weber, 1978). The consequences of these alienating transformations further incite the need to express oneself as a unique individual. This is well exemplified through an examination of how people use technology to fulfill this need.

Not only has our cultural preoccupation with ourselves been receiving much attention, but increasingly so in conjunction with discussions of the Internet. The Internet, by its very nature, not only facilitates the expression of individualism, it has increasingly been shaped by individuals for this purpose. The Internet consists of comprehensive networks that link its users and provide opportunities for interaction and expression through a variety of sites that are created and sustained by these users. The Internet  medium simultaneously provides opportunities for self-expression while supplying an audience to witness individual acts. Furthermore, expressions of individualism are not only performed for others, they are performed for the self; the Internet provides self-reflexive opportunities for individuals to construct and maintain one's uniqueness.

While the reasons people cite for using the Internet are many, it has increasingly become clear that the desire to express oneself as an autonomous and unique individual is an underlying motivation to participate in online interaction and communication. The following discussion will demonstrate the many ways in which the Internet facilitates individual expressions of self and the ways that people use sites on the Internet for that purpose.

> "The shift to a personalized, wireless world affords truly *personal communities* that supply support, sociability, information, and a sense of belonging separately to each individual" (Wellman, 2001).

Prior to a more applied discussion of the numerous sites and venues through which people are able to express their individualism, it is helpful to first outline the framework through which this occurs online. There has been a proposed shift in community organization and participation over the past several decades that is salient to this discussion. Sociologist Robert Putnam has

Christina Kalinowski

 noted a significant decline in community-based participation over the past 25 years. Participation in these organizations (i.e., labor unions) not only benefit the individual and the other members within that specific community, but can and do extend to benefit the wider community (i.e., by lobbying for better wages) (Putnam, 1995). Picking up where Putnam left off, sociologist Barry Wellman notes that we have shifted from conceptualizations of more traditional organizational-based communities to personal communities, meaning we organize our communities around ourselves, as opposed to group goals (Wellman, 2001). Thus, community has transitioned from solitary groups to individualized networks (Wellman, 2001; Matei, 2005). These personal communities emphasize individual autonomy and agency as each person controls and directly benefits from being the center of his or her own community (Wellman, 2001). The Internet has provided a context conducive to the construction and maintenance of personal communities and, hence, opportunities for individual expression.

The sheer amount of "massness," in addition to individual reactions to it, can be used to further our understanding of the Internet as a place favorable to individual expression. People are aware that, in larger society, they are considered members of a faceless mass (Weinberger, 2003). Understandably, this creates tension as we struggle to maintain our individualism among the "massness." The Internet, which presently consists of a mass of millions of individual users, provides a context that offers more opportunities than found offline to assert our individual uniqueness (Weinberger, 2003). Online we can create personal home pages, participate in discussion forums, and rate and review products and services, among other things. While a mass of individuals each asserting their individualism can have the unintentional effect of creating  "massness," Weinberger ultimately concludes that "the Web consists of a mass that refuses to lose its individual faces" (p. 115).

Weinberger draws on Amazon.com product reviews to exemplify this. He notes that, initially, individuals write reviews, which makes a person's opinion known to others. But as the number of reviews grows, what makes each opinion unique dissipates into "massness." Amazon.com has since implemented a simple yes or no rating scale that others can use to rate an individual reviewer's helpfulness. Users with highly rated reviews then stand out as, once again, unique (indeed this can be seen upon visiting Amazon.com and reading the 'Spotlight Reviews' of Weinberger's book!). We assert our individuality, and others aid us in our quest. As social creatures, we recognize that "our understanding and our behavior are shaped by the fact that there are other people" (Weinberger, 2003, p. 118). Because we feel impelled to assert our individualism amid the "massness," we understand why others feel the need to as well. The Internet thus facilitates interactions that allow us to participate amid our shared interests while still maintaining our individuality.

Attempts at resisting "massness" online can also be exemplified through an examination of marketing. Searls and Weinberger (2001) note that markets have undergone an historical shift, from a noun as a physical place (market) where customers could hold conversations with sellers and fellow customers about

 products, to a verb (marketing) that ends the conversation, casting customers as passive recipients of advertising messages. As a direct result, we have subsequently been massively lumped into faceless collectivities based upon superficial characteristics such as age, class, and race, which strips us of our individuality (Weinberger, 2003; Searls & Weinberger, 2001). Through online interactions we have a chance to regain our individuality by engaging in conversations with others and voicing our opinions about the products and services that are marketed to us (Searls & Weinberger, 2001). We don't appreciate the assumption that we can simply be lumped into a faceless aggregate, and we appreciate even less marketers' assumptions that we will buy their products based upon targeted, superficial characteristics. We each possess personal preferences and opinions about products; online, our unique experiences with certain products allow us to craft ourselves as knowledgeable, and to share this information with others.

This brief summarization on the nature of the Internet and how it facilitates the expression of individualism provides a background for a more applied discussion of the ways in which people express their individuality by using specific spaces on the Internet. This discussion will benefit from an examination of three popular online venues; 1) social network sites, 2) online communities, specifically the WELL, and 3) blogs. These three spaces are each indicative of processes that presently occur in cyberspace. Popular social network sites such as MySpace and Facebook are not only known by their members as sites for socialization and individual expression, scholars have observed that these sites have been responsible for shaping the larger business, cultural, and research landscape (Boyd & Ellison, 2007). The WELL has been heralded as one of the very first online communities and has been extensively examined by  numerous scholars; as Hafner (1997) notes, "History has decreed the WELL to be synonymous with online communication at its best, worst, and, above all, most vital forms" (p. 1). And lastly, blogs have come to represent the epitome of individual expression as a majority of blogs function as online diaries where people communicate personal information about themselves (Ringmar, 2007). While each of these venues differs in its own respective ways, each has been popularly used to convey one's individuality to others.

"Public displays of connection" (Donath & Boyd, 2004, as cited in Boyd & Ellison, 2007).

Social network sites provide a variety of ways for users to express themselves. Typical social network sites provide users with a home page or profile where one can "type oneself into being" (Sunden, 2003, as cited in Boyd & Ellison, 2007). People are provided with spaces in which they have the opportunity to communicate who they are and what their interests are to others. Furthermore, many social network sites provide seemingly limitless ways in which individuals can personalize their pages, thus making them more unique (Boyd & Ellison, 2007; Wellman, 2001). MySpace allows members to import backgrounds and add and arrange text, video, and pictures on one's profile. Similarly, Facebook allows outside developers to create "Applications" such as chart travel histories

 and "flair" that members can add to further personalize their profile. The ability to map the geographical locations one has visited and to express oneself through pins (icons) further allows one to distinguish one's individuality.

While social network sites like MySpace and Facebook are typically organized around people, usually people that a member has befriended or is acquainted with in real life, these sites also provide the opportunity for members to meet new people, and to interact with others based on shared interests (Boyd & Ellison, 2007). Who a member is friends with can tell us a lot about who a person is. As Donath and Boyd (2004) state these "public displays of connections serve as important identity signals that help people navigate the networked social world, in that an extended network may serve to validate identity information presented in profiles" (as cited in Boyd & Ellison, 2007). Whether we join social networking sites to maintain contact with friends and family or to meet others (or both), public displays of our networks simultaneously allow us to signal who we are to others while providing information that corroborates our expressions of individuality.

"You Own Your Words" (WELL motto).

The WELL has popularly been conceptualized as a virtual community (Rheingold, 1993). Technically speaking, the WELL is an asynchronous, non-anonymous bulletin board that consists of a wide array of topic "conferences" that members can read and contribute to (Rheingold, 1993). In his influential book *The Virtual Community: Homesteading on the Electronic*

126

Frontier, Rheingold (1993) presents his personal investigations of the WELL, which, due largely to his history of active involvement, frame the WELL as an unrealistically utopian virtual community. Not surprisingly, his  depiction has been heavily contested (Hafner, 1997; Matei, 2005; Rheingold, 2001). Upon revisiting his work years later, Rheingold (2001) realized the erroneous judgments he had made, removed his rose-tinted spectacles, and revised some of his original statements. Rheingold ultimately came to the realization that not everyone shared his amicable feelings toward the WELL by considering themselves a part of a community; for many, the WELL primarily functioned as a place conducive to self-expression (Hafner, 1997; Matei, 2005; Rheingold, 2001).

John Seabrook, in writing about his tentative excursions into the WELL in his book *Deeper*, arrived at the same conclusion; the WELL was not so much a community but rather a place for members to draw attention to themselves (Seabrook, 1997; Matei, 2005). Many members of the WELL themselves mirror this sentiment. Matei (2005), in examining members' responses to the query "Is the WELL a community?" found that many framed their answers in terms of autonomy, individualism, and self-interest. This can be likened to the concept of networked individualism in that, for many, participation on the WELL served as a personal community through which members directly benefited from being the center of their own community (Wellman, 2001).

The very motto of the WELL, "you own your words," constructs the WELL as an open space in which members are free to express their individuality. Once

 members post to "conferences" their contributions are saved so that they and others may visit and re-visit them, effectively preserving member's carefully constructed expressions of self. Well, that is, until some of the higher-ups created a tool capable of mass deletions and placed it in the wrong hands (Hafner, 1997). Members of the WELL received quite the surprise one day when Tom Mandel, a WELL authority and resident eccentric known for his unstable personality, deleted the entire "Future" and "Weird" conferences; as a result, years of conversation were eradicated (Hafner, 1997). Members expressed shock, dismay, and outrage; needless to say, they were upset. And why shouldn't they have been? Many members had spent years expressing themselves on the WELL only to have many of their individual contributions erased. This act of deletion not only discredited the WELL's motto, it was a direct attack on members' freedom of expression.

"...on the Web, everyone will be famous to fifteen people" (Weinberger, 2002).

The expression of individualism appears most evident in the act of blogging. Blogs can be likened to journal entries in that they are usually produced by an individual author for the purpose of personal expression (Ringmar, 2007). While the contents of blogs may vary across those who create and maintain them, the point is that blogs provide a personal space for individuals to have their voices heard (Kornblum, 2003). As such, blogs are designed with an audience in mind (Blood, 2003; Ringmar, 2007). Blogs allow individual voices to be heard amid the "massness"; they

128

have allowed us to enter the conversation once again (Blood, 2003; Kornblum, 2003, Searls & Weinberger, 2001).

But blogs function as more than just individual segues back into the conversation; they are interactive extensions of who we are (Blood, 2003). Eric Ringmar (2007) echoes this when he says that "a blog is ourselves in cyberspace" (p. 14). Common responses given when bloggers are queried as to their reasons for blogging include the need to express oneself creatively, to document personal experiences, to voice opinions, and to leave a record of having been there (Hewitt, 2002; Ringmar, 2007), all of which are highly individual-centered reasons for participation in blogging activities. Blogs are, more than anything else, a means by which we describe and explain our lives to ourselves; as such, blogging is a self-reflexive activity (Ringmar, 2007).

Current and widely valued conceptions of individualism require an individual to self-reflexively engage oneself, and blogs provide an advantageous context for doing so (Ringmar, 2007). Blogs are spaces that enable us to write ourselves into existence. Seabrook (2002) made the observation that "written words seem to have a more symbolic relationship to your thoughts and emotions... you are a kind of mental nudist" (p. 177). People often reveal personal life details online that they never would offline. Thus it is no surprise that researchers have found that we tend to feel more confident and comfortable expressing and self-reflexively exploring ourselves online (McKenna & Bargh, 2000). Such explorations, which can meet with resistance offline by one's peers, can be effortlessly examined in front of our online audience(s) (McKenna

Christina Kalinowski

 & Bargh, 2000). We need to express ourselves and be recognized by others before we can be someone; identity creation requires an audience and, online, there is always someone watching (Ringmar, 2007). Thus, blogs, and the Internet medium itself, assist us in the exploration of self and expression of individualism.

"The WELL seems to be all about self-expression, not communication. Expression is a solitary activity – like shouting in the forest, perhaps I should say electrovoid. I have a picture in my mind's eye of the WELL – actually, of about fifty little wells – each one sunk deep into rock; each one perfectly insulated from every other one; and at the bottom of each, a person with a keyboard, furiously and fruitlessly hammering away" (comment from a WELL member, as cited in Matei, 2005).

While individualism is clearly a primary motivation for people to use the Internet, sites for self-expression are not without tension. Even though the Internet is a medium that facilitates greater freedom of individual self-expression and self-reflexivity, there are still conflicts inherent in using online venues to convey individualism. With respect to the WELL, many users, like the one cited above, were keenly aware of the persistent tension that exists between individual and communitarian ideals (Matei, 2005). The WELL was "founded as a self-conscious virtual community and proclaimed itself as such" (Rheingold, 1987, as cited in Matei, 2005), while simultaneously proclaiming to uphold the freedom of expression (Matei, 2005).

However, it should be noted that this ideal of freedom of expression does not mean that one can say whatever one wants and pass it off as "expressing my individualism"; the WELL, initially founded without

http://ubimark.com/in/books/584/

filters on the premise that everyone had a right to be heard, eventually developed community guidelines that members were expected to adhere to. This culminated when Mark Ethan Smith, a radical and controversial  personality who began lashing out and personally attacking WELL members, was the first person to be booted from the WELL (Hafner, 1997). It only takes one to ruin it for everyone. As a result of this and similar incidents, the new understanding of the WELL was that members were granted the freedom of speech and expression insofar as it didn't impinge on other members' freedoms. Repeated violations of this understanding leave an offender susceptible to deletion. Members had come to the realization that since self-expression is a solitary activity, and that since their discourse was being articulated in a community setting, they had to strike a compromise between the desire to be heard and being respectful of others. Participation in the WELL thus required members to deal with the tension between these two conflicting ideals.

These and other tensions are present in other online spaces as well. Blogs, which are primarily conceptualized by their owners as spaces where they are free to say what they want and have their voices heard, are not liberated from these constraints. Blogs are not just isolated, free-floating entities; blogs must co-exist with other blogs. And there are norms that bloggers are expected to follow. For instance, it is expected that bloggers will credit one another when borrowing information by providing links to the original source of that information (Blood, 2003).

And the same rules apply concerning what you can and cannot say, just like on the WELL; not only could

Christina Kalinowski

 what you say (or forget to say!) get you in trouble with your online peers, but it could also have real world consequences. Eric Ringmar found this out the hard way when he was pressured to resign from his tenured professorial position at the London School of Economics due to things he posted about the university and staff in his personal blog (Ringmar, 2007). Similarly, strings of "Facebook firings" have recently been generating controversy over whether or not employers should be allowed to fire employees based on the content of their profiles. One casualty, sixteen-year-old Kimberley Swann, found this out the hard way when her employers sacked her for publishing status updates that stated how boring her job was, even though she never revealed the name of her place of employment (Pothen, 2009).

It has become apparent that the Internet has increasingly been portrayed and perceived as a utopian space, where individuals can be free to express themselves and have their voices heard. However, as many who have flocked to the Internet have discovered, the Internet is not the exactly the place they envisioned it to be. While the Internet has been designed to facilitate the expression of individualism by its users, there are limits to how far we can go. Online is not so different from offline, as many otherwise purport it to be. Our online interactions can (and do) have offline consequences. While one may feel freer to express oneself and be more confident in doing so on the Internet, our rights to free expression are just as limited online as they are off. Expressions of individualism come with a price tag; such expressions are individual activities and serve to isolate and distance ourselves

from others. We need to be aware of how we choose to express ourselves, lest we forget that even though each of us are truly unique, we are social creatures and share the world with others who are just like us. As such, we need to keep in mind that social norms regarding respect for others do not cease to exist just because we log on.

People are increasingly taking note of the contradictory expectations inherent in using the Internet, and these tentative observations should be more fully explored. The idea that the offline world is significantly different from the online world undoubtedly has an influence upon individual behaviors. As social creatures, we have made the Internet a social medium which makes the study of online behaviors worthwhile. Having said that, research needs to be focused offline as well as on in order for us to more adequately comprehend the perceptions people hold regarding online environments and they ways in which they use them to navigate the tension between individualism and socially constructed norms regarding respect for others.

References

Bellah, R., Madsen, R., Sullivan, W., Swidler, A., & Tipton, S. (2008). Habits of the Heart: Individualism and Commitment in American Life. Berkeley, CA: University of California Press.

Blood, R. (Author), & Editors of Perseus Publishing (Eds.). (2002). We've Got Blog: How Weblogs are Changing our Culture. Cambridge: Perseus Publishing.

 Boyd, D., & Ellison, N. (2007). Social Network Sites: Definition, History, and Scholarship. Journal of Computer Mediated Communication, 13(1), article 11.

Hafner, K. (1997). The Epic Saga of the WELL. Wired, 5(5). Retrieved from http://www.wired.com/wired/archive/5.05/ff_well_pr.html

Hewitt, H. (2005). Blog: Understanding the Information Reformation that's Changing Your World. Nashville, TN: Nelson Books.

Kornblum, J. (2003). Welcome to the Blogosphere. USA Today. Retrieved from http://www.usatoday.com/tech/webguide/internetlife/2003-07-08-blogs_x.htm

Matei, S. (2005). From Counterculture to Cyberculture: Virtual Community Discourse and the Dilemma of Modernity. Journal of Computer-Mediated Communication, 10(3).

McKenna, K., & Bargh, J. (2000). Plan 9 From Cyberspace: The Implications of the Internet for Personality and Social Psychology. Personality and Social Psychology Review, 4, 57-75.

Pothen, J. (2009, March 5). Facebook-Induced Firing. The Cornell Daily Sun.

Putnam, R. (2001). Bowling Alone: The Collapse and Revival of American Community. New York: Simon and Schuster.

Rheingold, H. (1993). The Virtual Community: Homesteading on the Electronic Frontier (1st ed.). Cambridge: MIT Press.

Rheingold, H. (2001). The Virtual Community: Homesteading on the Electronic Frontier (Rev. ed.). Cambridge: MIT Press.

Ringmar, E. (2007). A Blogger's Manifesto: Free Speech and Censorship in the Age of the Internet. London: Anthem Press.

Individualism Online

http://ubimark.com/in/books/584/

Seabrook, J. (1997). Deeper: My Two-Year Odyssey in Cyberspace. New York: Simon and Schuster.

Locke, C., Levine, R., Searls, D., & Weinberger, D. (2001). The Cluetrain Manifesto: The End of Business as Usual. Cambridge: Basic Books.

Weber, M. (Author), & Runciman, W. G. (Ed.). (1978). Max Weber: Selections in Translation. Cambridge: Cambridge University Press.

Weinberger, D. (2003). Small Pieces Loosely Joined. Cambridge: Basic Books.

Wellman, B. (2001). Physical Place and CyberPlace: The Rise of Personalized Networking. International Journal of Urban and Regional Research, 25, 227-252.

SIDE Theory, Small World Networks, and Smart Mob Formation: A Beginner's Guide

W. Scott Sanders

Http://ubimark.com/in/books/585/

Abstract

Despite the great potential smart mobs (ad-hoc social networks) have to impact how business and politics are conducted, very little effort has been expended to explore the cognitive precursors that would motivate individuals to participate. This paper presents a theoretical explanation for smart mob behavior rooted in shared social identity and fostered by the structural characteristics of the supporting technologies. Drawing upon real-life examples, this paper suggests necessary prerequisites and favorable conditions for the formation of ad-hoc mobile networks.

Over the past two decades the introduction of new communication technologies has changed how individuals interact with one another. The popularization of the Internet encouraged the creation of online wiki communities in which all users have the ability to create, reorder, and edit content in such a way that no one person can be identified as the author of the final, and often continually evolving, piece. Likewise, blogging has taken publishing out of the hands of a few select gatekeepers and has allowed any individual with access to the Internet to publish their own thoughts and opinions. Mobile phones have allowed individuals to reorder their lives and coordinate actions in a previously impossible manner. This availability of many-to-many forms of communication creates a necessary condition for the production of smart mobs, mobile ad hoc social networks, which are the result of individuals using personal communication technologies to coordinate collective action. Smart  mobs seem to share at least some characteristics with the emergent behavior of swarm systems (Rheingold, 2002). However, there is one important difference between characteristic swarming behavior and that of smart mobs; individual human beings have considerable intellect. While there are several documented examples of smart mobs displaying emergent behavior, it is most important to consider the cognitive mechanisms and the network structures that create the prerequisite conditions for smart mob formation.

Smart mobs have been documented in a number of different contexts. An exemplar of smart mob behavior is the 2001 toppling of the Estrada administration in the Philippines when citizens were urged to take to the streets wearing black (Bociurkiw, 2001; Rheingold, 2002). A more recent example is the French race riots of the summer of 2005 during which police revealed that rioting teenagers were using the Internet and short message service (SMS) messages to coordinate attacks (Smith, 2005). Likewise, during December of 2005 Australia had to contend with youth using SMS messages to instigate and coordinate violence aimed at individuals of Middle Eastern descent in response to the beating of two lifeguards (BBC, 2005).

Although incompatible networks initially hampered their adoption in the United States, many countries have long had a booming SMS trend because of its relative cheapness compared to phone calls. SMS messages have

 proven an important mechanism in the development of smart mobs for several reasons. First, SMS is an asynchronous communication that allows its users to exert more cognitive effort on expressing and editing thoughts. Second, technological constraints force messages to be brief and to the point allowing them to be created and sent quickly. SMS technology allows brief written messages of a maximum of 160 characters to be sent and received via mobile phones (Featherly, 2003). Furthermore, messages can be sent or forwarded to everyone in an individual's address book. This is allows a message to be disseminated more quickly than a traditional phone tree where each individual would have to be contacted separately, thereby allowing large networks to be mobilized relatively quickly (Walker, 2003). Finally, SMS messages are sent to mobile phones rather than email inboxes or hard lines. One of the mobile phone's primary functions is to serve as a coordination tool. Mobile phones allow micro-coordination of behavior by allowing for midcourse adjustments and the softening of time where the timing of schedules and events are negotiated or reordered (Ling, 2004; Ling & Yttri, 2002).

One explanation for the creation of smart mobs is the threshold models of collective behavior. Threshold models propose that individuals have a particular threshold at which they are willing to engage in collective action (Granovetter, 1978). Threshold models attempt to explain why individuals may be willing to participate in actions collectively that they would not be willing to participate in alone. The argument hinges upon individuals conducting a cost-benefit analysis that weighs the rewards of engaging in the behavior against the possible repercussions. The more people that choose to participate in particular actions the less likely an individual will be held accountable for their behavior. Some individuals require very few individuals to  participate prior to joining in, while others may wait for a majority of the population to engage in a behavior before taking action. Furthermore, since the threshold is simply the point at which an individual chooses to engage in a behavior, two individuals whose thresholds are the same may not be politically identical, as reflected in the popular expression "strange bedfellows" (Granovetter, 1978, pp. 1422). In short, individuals do not have to share the same motivation to engage in a behavior, they merely must have their threshold level met.

Although the threshold theory holds that individuals need not share an ideology for collective action, Ling (2004) notes "these social aggregates [smart mobs] function as a unit so long as there is a shared ideology and a common sense of strategy, and so long as there is a focused easily communicated form of interaction" (p. 187). Therefore, rather than individuals merely having a threshold that must be exceeded in order to take action, individuals in smart mobs may require a shared sense of identity. Social identity deindividuation theory (SIDE) was developed to explain online group interaction through people's identification with social identities. Its basic tenet is that text based environments, such as the Internet, served to limit nonverbal cues so that individuals are deindividuated (Walther & Parks, 2002). Deindividuation is the loss of self-awareness and critical evaluation of actions as a result of the anonymity created by group scenarios. For example, larger group

W. Scott Sanders

 sizes have been found to facilitate behavior that contradicts societal norms such as taunting suicides to jump or joining a lynch mob (Mann, 1981; Mullen, 1986). Furthermore, anonymity under conditions of deindividuation has been found to result in salience given to contextual cues concerning how to behave (Johnson & Downing, 1979; Spivey & Prentice-Dunn, 1990). Considered in the context of communication media, it has been found that different media may result in the personal and social attributes being more or less salient. For example, individuated individuals, who were placed in the same room as one another during interaction, were less likely to comply with group norms and more likely to exert an independent identity (Postmes, Spears, & Lea, 1998). Deindividuation in turn affects whether interpersonal or intergroup differences matter during interaction (Postmes & Baym, 2005).

When people cannot individuate others they are forced to rely on contextual cues that indicate the social identities of group members. Social identities do not just consist of an individual's understanding of a group or social category, but are a shared conception within a group of the defining features of group membership (Postmes & Baym, 2005). Along with norms, social identity can mold group action as a result of social identification and social categorization. Social identification is the internalization of a social identity resulting from long term identification with a particular group and so that group norms are subsequently adopted as personal norms. Conversely, categorization is the result of social context increasing the salience of particular social categories. In short, rather than relating to others as individuals, SIDE theory proposes

that, in conditions of limited information and subsequent deindividuation, people relate to one another on the basis of group membership.
Initially, it seems unlikely that SIDE theory can provide an explanation of group behavior in smart mobs. First, individuals who receive a message calling for a smart mob to coalesce may know the sender. After all, the primary way that smart mob messages spread is via forwarded messages sent to multiple receivers in the sender's address book. The key rests in the receiver's media literacy. It is common for received text messages to be forwarded to others in some cultures, for example, teen cultures of Asian and Scandinavian countries. If individuals perceive the message as originating from the immediate sender, then SIDE effects probably will not be observed because too much individuating information is known about the sender. That is, the receiver is more likely to relate to the sender on an interpersonal level rather than a group level. However, if the receiver interprets the message as a call for action that has not originated from the immediate sender then it is possible that they will identify with the message on a group level and respond to the cues embedded in the message.

SMS technology may be highly conducive to producing anonymous messages that can be used to galvanize support for causes and make calls for action. For example, during the SARS crisis of spring 2003, SMS messages circulated in China satirically poking fun at government officials and protocols and urging individuals to stock up on rice and salt (Yu, 2004). The events in China highlight the subversive potential of SMS as a tool for protest. The anonymity afforded the

W. Scott Sanders

 initial composer of a message and those who forwarded it can be used to oppose powerful social institutions from a safe distance. Furthermore, the text-based nature of SMS, along with its limitations on the number of characters a message can contain make it an extremely lean medium which may contribute to the activation of a social identity rather than an individual identity.

The second factor that interferes with the application of SIDE theory to smart mobs is that many smart mobs do not have a great deal of interaction. Social identity is formed not only from "common perspectives of group history and a sense of future direction but most importantly through comparison and differentiation from relevant outgroups" (Postmes & Baym, 2005, pp. 224). This process of developing a group identity through the creation of a shared history and comparison to outgroups is accomplished by individuals using the content of others messages to create and strengthen group norms (Walther & Parks, 2002). However, this presents a quandary in the context of smart mobs that may have little interaction prior to the initial call to action. Even if a receiver contacted the immediate sender of a forwarded message, the sender likely would be unable to assist them in identifying others who might have received the same message outside of their own personal contacts.

Rather than developing a social identity through mediated interaction, it is possible that individuals who respond to the initiating message of a smart mob already possess a salient social identity that was formed during everyday interaction in their society. It should be noted that the best documented occurrences of smart mob behavior are in contexts such as political dissent,

race riots, and celebrity stalking.
Individuals who are involved in these
activities may already have preformed
identities that are activated by the
reception of a SMS message.

Postmes and Baym (2005) have noted
that an individual's social identity can be made salient
by features of the social context that do not require the
presence of other group members. Therefore, social
categorization may often prove to be an incredibly
powerful dynamic in determining the actions of
individuals in a smart mob. However, information
provided via SMS messages activates social
categorizations only when contextual cues make that
information salient to the individuals. For example, an
individual who is a fan of a certain movie star may
receive a text message urging them to converge on a
location at which the star has been seen. If they are
close by and the detour costs them little time and effort,
the individual may be more likely to follow the
message's suggestion than if they are across town and
would be required to expend considerable time and
effort to do so. The message coupled with proximity
provides contextual cues that activate the social identity
of a fan. Likewise, events may also provoke social
categorization. For example, the attack on two
lifeguards at Cronulla beach in Sydney, Australia by
youths perceived to be of Lebanese descent may have
increased the salience of ethnic identity to the point that
white youth could be mobilized via SMS messages.

Now that we have considered the cognitive
mechanisms that may lead individuals to participate in
smart mobs, it is also important to consider the network
structure that allows smart mobs to form. Specifically,
small world networks may be an essential component of

W. Scott Sanders

 the development of smart mobs. Small world networks were first proposed in the 1950's in an effort to estimate the number of links required to connect any two individuals living within the United States (Monge & Contractor, 2003). By considering the full range of an individual's social contacts they concluded that two to three others would link the majority of individuals. Stanley Milgram, who asked individuals in Nebraska and Kansas to send a letter to Boston via intermediaries, tested this conclusion in 1967. Half of the letters were received after going through no more than five individuals.

Several types of networks have the potential to form in the real world. Small world networks are characterized by a high degree of clustering among local nodes with a few far-flung links to distant nodes so that all nodes are separated by no more than a few links (Monge & Contractor, 2003). Regular networks consist of nodes with a few links to only their immediate neighbors. While regular networks demonstrate high degrees of clustering, nodes may be separated by numerous links. Finally, random networks exist where the nodes are randomly linked. Random networks lack clustering but do have a low degree of separation between nodes. Watts (1999, as cited in Monge & Contractor, 2003) believes that small world networks, rather than regular or random networks, comprise a majority of networks found in the real world.

Small world networks have important implications for the formation and function of smart mobs. Small world networks help explain how smart mobs form quickly. Milgram's experiment shows that human social networks are, or at least approximate, small world networks. Smart mobs are initiated via text messages

144

sent to multiple individuals in the sender's address book and, therefore, can be considered a subset of an individual's social network. Still, the majority of people who the immediate sender of a smart mob SMS knows are  likely not included in his address book. This limited list of contacts still may be sufficient to result in a small world network. Although lower link density between individuals in the network might inhibit the spread of an SMS, the nature of SMS technology, which forwards of the messages to large groups of people quickly, could counteract this by allowing for quick and efficient message transmission. There are currently approximately 2 billion mobile phones on the planet and many individuals who do not have access to other forms of new media, such as the Internet, that allow many-to-many communication own mobile phones (Gunn, personal communication). Such was the case in the Philippines during the 2001 protests against President Estrada. Much of the population lives in poverty and SMS provides a cheap, convenient method of communication (Bociurkiw, 2001). Although mobile phones were far from ubiquitous, small world social networks were likely a decisive factor in allowing messages calling for protest to quickly spread.

We must also take into consideration other mechanisms that effect network structure and the transmission of information. Proximity of nodes to one another may be especially important. When considering personal networks nodes are not chosen randomly but are "inversely proportional to the square of its geographical distance from the originating node" (Monge & Contractor, 2003, pp. 312). In other words, the closer two nodes are to one another the more likely

W. Scott Sanders

 they are to form a connection. Proximity is not only important for creating new connections but it also plays an important role in the maintenance and dissolution of established ones. Another factor that likely plays a role in transmission of messages to initiate a smart mob is homophily, or the extent to which individuals are similar. When homophily and proximity are jointly taken into account, individuals are much more effective in reaching their intended target with a message.

Both proximity and homophily may provide partial explanations of how smart mobs form. If mobile phone address books are merely subsets of our social networks, then small world network structures that take into account proximity suggests that a bulk of message recipients will be geographically proximal. This is important because smart mobs gather relatively quickly. Proximal individuals would be able to reasonably travel to the appointed destination without undue effort. Furthermore, this structure also suggests that individuals who would be constrained from participating in smart mobs by geographical distance would be less likely to receive the initiating message. Of course, proximities constraints on smart mob participation likely play little role in online smart mobs. Homophily may also play an important role in the spread of the initial smart mob message. If individuals are more likely to form social linkages with others that they perceive to be similar to themselves then individuals whose social identity is activated by a message are more likely to pass along that message to others than those who do not share that social identity. Not only would homophily facilitate the dissemination

http://ubimark.com/in/books/585/

of messages but it might also act as a filtering mechanism to prevent people to whom the message would be irrelevant from receiving it. People who do not identify with the message may be less likely to pass the message on to  others. As a result, the message is spread among those for whom it activates a social identity, and disregarded by those for whom it does not.

Ling (2004) notes that smart mobs are anomalies in the larger picture of mobile communication and arise only under specific conditions. First, he noted the social contextual features that promote a common ideology are necessary to develop the desire to take action. He illustrates this by showing how dissatisfaction with the corrupt Estrada regime in the Philippines predisposed individuals to protest. Second, he focused on the necessity of a clear, concise strategy for spurring action. Philippine citizens were encouraged to go to a well-known, symbolic location to engage in protest. Finally, he describes that the necessity of SMS as an easy and efficient channel for the spread of the initiating messages. Messages were forwarded via the protestors address books to others who might respond.

SIDE theory and small world networks fit neatly into this framework of the necessary preconditions for initiating a smart mob. First, individuals must have the necessary social identity for a smart mob to form. People will not respond to any message, just the ones that they feel are relevant to them. Second, while the social identities that could potentially lead to a smart mob likely persist over time, the social climate must be exact in order for smart mobs to develop. Social identities must be activated via the process of social-categorization by contextual features in the

W. Scott Sanders

 environment or by interaction with others. Additionally, others do not have to be present for this to occur. Contextual cues, such as the beating of the lifeguards at Cronulla beach, increase the salience of social identities so that they can potentially be activated by an SMS calling for specific action. It is for this reason that smart mobs are relatively uncommon. Finally, the nature of social networks as small world networks coupled with SMS technology is essential to the development of smart mobs. SMS provides a method for alerting many people simultaneously to the call for the formation of a smart mob. Small world network structures facilitate the spread by allowing messages to be received by individual nodes with a minimal number of linkages. The combination of these factors allows smart mobs to form instantaneously. Further network mechanisms serve to filter and promote the spread of initiating messages.

Smart mobs have been used purposefully to accomplish tasks impossible for a single hierarchical organization. Many of the same conditions that allow smart mobs to form also create conditions in which they can display emergent behavior. First, the nature of many-to-many communication mediums means that leadership is decentralized. This means that disabling one node in the network will not cripple it. A notable example of this is the Direct Action Network that used mobile communication devices to coordinate protest of the World Trade Organization in Seattle. Arresting "ring leaders" did not slow the attacks or seriously hamper coordination of efforts (de Armond, 2000). Second, human beings are autonomous and make the choice to submerge their personal identity in favor of a social one.

http://ubimark.com/in/books/585/

Furthermore, as individuals they have street level data and do not have an overall picture of the scenario. The conciseness of text messages mean that complex strategies cannot be laid out in detail but must evolve as events unfold.  Finally, the high connectivity provided by SMS technology allows individuals to coordinate action by converging on a target from many directions and then dispersing just as quickly. This phenomenon has been labeled "warming" in the contexts of political protests (Ronfeldt & Arquilla, 2001) but can also be observed in contexts as diverse as celebrity watching or article editing on Wikipedia. As a result of the role peer influence plays in a smart mob, the network structure of a smart mob, and the high connectivity that characterizes it, smart mobs can be highly adaptive and unpredictable.

The application of SIDE theory to mobile ad hoc mobile networks helps illustrate how difficult, if not impossible, it would be to intentionally start a smart mob if the prerequisite conditions were not in place. When the conditions are right it may be possible to initiate and determine the initial trajectory of a smart mobs actions, but then it takes a life of its own. However, starting a smart mob from scratch may be impossible. A man pleaded in a comment left on the Smart Mob blog, "Help Im [sic] running for polictical [sic] office, and i [sic] want to use this method to reach the voters who are on the net. how [sic] do I go about doing this.[sic]" (Rheingold & Grayman, 2003). Appropriately, he never received a response.

VIRTUAL SOCIABILITY

W. Scott Sanders

References

BBC News. (2005). Howard condemns riots in Sydney. Retrieved May 2, 2006, from http://news.bbc.co.uk/1/hi/world/asia-pacific/4520218.stm

Bociurkiw, M. (2001). Revolution by Cell Phone. Retrieved May 2, 2006, from http://www.forbes.com/asap/2001/0910/028.html

de Armond, P. (2000). Black Flag Over Seattle. Retrieved May 2, 2006, from http://www.monitor.net/monitor/seattlewto/index.html

Featherly, K. (2003). Short Messaging System. In S. Jones (Ed.), Encyclopedia of New Media (pp. 408-411). Thousand Oaks, CA: Sage.

Granovetter, M. (1978). Threshold models of collective behavior. American Journal of Sociology, 83(6), 1420-1443.

Johnson, R. W., & Downing, L. J. (1979). Deindividuation and valence of cues: Effects of prosocial and antisocial behavior. Journal of Personality and Social Psychology, 37, 1532-1538.

Ling, R. (2004). The Mobile Connection: The Cell Phone's Impact on Society. San Francisco, Elsevier.

Ling, R. and Yttri, B. (2002). Hyper-coordination Via mobile phones in Norway. In J. E. Katz & M. Aakhus (Eds.), Perpetual Contact: Mobile Communication, Private Talk, Public Performance (pp. 139-169). Cambridge: Cambridge University Press.

Mann, L. (1981). The baiting crowd in episodes of threatened suicide. Journal of Personality and Social Psychology, 55, 703-709.

Monge, P. R., & Contractor, N. (2003).-Theories of Communication Networks.-New York: Oxford University Press.

SIDE Theory

Mullen, B. (1986). Atrocity as a function of lynch mob composition: A self--attention perspective. Personality and Social Psychology Bulletin, 12, 187-197.

Postmes, T., & Baym, N. (2005). Intergroup dimensions of the Internet. In J. Harwood & H. Giles (Eds.), Intergroup communication: Multiple perspectives (pp. 213-238). New York: Peter Lang.

Postmes, T., Spears, R., & Lea M. (1998). Breaching or building social boundaries? side-effects of computer-mediated communication. Communication Research, 25(6), 689-715.

Rheingold , H. (2002). Smart mobs: The next social revolution. Cambridge, MA: Perseus.

Rheingold, H. and Grayman. (2003). Smartmobs Sway Korean Elections? Retrieved May 2, 2006, from http://www.smartmobs.com/archive/2002/12/23/smartmobs_sway_.html

Ronfeldt, D., and Arquilla, J. (2001). Networks, netwars, and the fight for the Future. Retrieved May 2, 2006, from http://www.firstmonday.org/issues/issue6_10/ronfeldt/index.html

Spivey, C.B., & Prentice-Dunn, S. (1990). Assessing the directionality of deindividuated behavior: Effects of deindividuation, modeling, and private self-consciousness on aggressive and prosocial responses. Basic and Applied Social Psychology, 11, 387-403.

Walker, J. (2003). Is That a Computer in Your Pants? Reason, 34, 36-42.

Walther, J. B., & Parks, M. R. (2002). Cues filtered out, cues filtered in: Computer-mediated communication and relationships. In M. L. Knapp & J. A. Daly (Eds.), Handbook of interpersonal communication (3rd ed., pp. 529-563). Thousand Oaks, CA: Sage.

VIRTUAL SOCIABILITY

W. Scott Sanders

Watts, D.J. (1999). Small worlds: The dynamics of networks between order and randomness. Princeton, NJ: Princeton University Press.

Yu, H. (2004). The power of thumbs: The politics of sms in urban China. Graduate Journal of Asia-Pacific Studies, 2(2), 30-43.

Online Interaction: Selected Readings and Discussion Topics

http://ubimark.com/in/books/1000

The big picture: Origins
- **What is the WELL? What are its ideals?**
- **What seems to motivate on-line participation on the WELL?**
- **What is the difference between Seabrook's and Rheingold's vision about the benefits (costs) of on-line communities?**

1. Rheingold, H. (2001). *The Virtual Community: Homesteading on the electronic frontier* (1st HarperPerennial ed.). New York, NY: HarperPerennial.
   - Read Introduction, Ch. 1-2

2. Seabrook, J. (1997). *Deeper.* New York, NY: Simon & Schuster.

3. Hafner, K. (1997, May). The epic saga of the Well. *Wired, 5*(5). Retrieved from http://www.wired.com/wired/archive/5.05/ff_well.html

USEFUL: Those curious to see with their own eyes where it all started can visit www.well.com or www.theriver.com, a spin-off of the Well.

Also informative: Hauben, M. (1995). Netizens. On the history and the impact of the net. Retrieved from http://www.columbia.edu/~hauben/netbook

 **Virtual communities and the promise of "communitas"**
- **What is "communitas"?**
- **Are virtual communities "communitas"-like environments? In what way?**
- **What rituals characterize online communities, at least as these are described by Rheingold or Seabrook?**
- **What is the relationship between equality and communitas?**

1. Turner, E. (2004). Rites of communitas. In F. A. Salamone (Ed.), *Encyclopedia of religious rites, rituals, and festivals* (pp. 97–101). New York: Routledge.

2. Turner, V. (1995). *The Ritual Process*. Chicago: Aldine.

3. Deflem, M. (1991). Ritual, Anti-Structure, and Religion: A Discussion of Victor Turner's Processual Symbolic Analysis. *Journal for the Scientific Study of Religion, 30*(1), 1-25.

4. Waskul, D. D. (2005). Ekstasis and the Internet: liminality and computer-mediated communication. *New Media and Society, 7*(1), 47-63.

5. Lawless, E. J. (1998). Ars Rhetorica en Communitas: Reclaiming the Voice of Passionate Expression in Electronic Writing. *Rhetoric Review, 16*(2), 310-326.

Individuality, subjectivity and community: Is there a connection?

- **Why does Weinberger say that "the web is for community"?**
- **Is the web a space for personal realization? Or only for personal self-realization?**
- **Is Weinberger closer to Rheingold or to Seabrook? Or to neither?**

1. Weinberger, D. (2002). *Small pieces loosely joined.* Cambridge, MA: Perseus.
   - Read Ch. 5-6

2. Levine, R., Locke, C., Searls, D., & Weinberger, D. (2001). *The Cluetrain Manifesto.* New York, NY: Perseus.
   - Read Markets are Conversations, Hyperlinked Organization

Individuality, subjectivity, community applied – social media
- **What is the social impulse behind blogging?**
- **Can it be explained in terms of networked individualism (Wellman), subjective appropriation of knowledge (Weinberger) or as a tension between individualism and communitarianism (Matei)?**
- **Will blogging lead to the ultimate demise of traditional forms of communication/journalism?**

1. boyd, d. m., & Ellison, N. B. (2007). Social network sites: Definition, history, and

 scholarship. *Journal of Computer-Mediated Communication, 13*(1), article 11.

2. Wolf, G. (2004). How the Internet Invented Howard Dean. *Wired, 12*(1). Retrieved from http://www.wired.com/wired/archive/12.01/dean.html

3. Kornblum, J. (2003, July 8). Welcome to the Blogosphere. *USA Today*. Retrieved from http://www.usatoday.com/tech/webguide/internetlife/2003-07-08-blogs_x.htm

4. Madden, A. (2005, August). The Business of Blogging. *Technology Review*. Retrieved from http://www.technologyreview.com/business/14653

OPTIONAL: Gillmor, D. (2004). *We the Media.* Sebastopol, CA: O'Reilly.

Individuality, subjectivity, community applied – wikis
- **What is wiki? What is mass collaboration?**
- **How can we best describe Wikipedia?**
- **What are its main strengths?**
- **Weaknesses?**
- **How does Wikipedia fit in our discussion so far?**

1. Bloomberg. (2007). The BusinessWeek Wikinomics Series. Retrieved from http://www.businessweek.com/innovate/di_special/wikinomics.htm

2. Wikipedia. (2011). Wikipedia: Neutral point of view. Retrieved February 6, 2011 from http://en.wikipedia.org/wiki/Wikipedia:Neutral_point_of_view

3. McHenry, R. (2004, November 15). The Faith-Based Encyclopedia [Web log comment]. Message posted to http://www.ideasinactiontv.com/tcs_daily/2004/11/the-faith-based-encyclopedia.html

4. Schiff, S. (2006, July). Know it all. *The New Yorker*. Retrieved from http://www.newyorker.com/archive/2006/07/31/060731fa_fact

5. Sjöberg, L. (2006, April 19). The Wikipedia FAQK. *Wired*. Retrieved from http://www.wired.com/software/webservices/commentary/alttext/2006/04/70670

6. Kittur, A., Chi, E., Pendelton, B. A., Suh, B., & Mytkowicz, T. (2007). *Power of the Few vs. Wisdom of the Crowd: Wikipedia and the Rise of the Bourgeoisie*. Retrieved from http://www.viktoria.se/altchi/submissions/submission_edchi_1.pdf

7. Matei, S. A., & Dobrescu, C. (2006, June). *Ambiguity and conflict in the Wikipedian knowledge production system*. Paper presented at the 56th Annual Conference of the International Communication Association, Dresden, Germany.

 BROWSE:
- Wikipedia. (2011). Statistics. Retrieved February 6, 2011 from http://en.wikipedia.org/wiki/Special:Statistics

- Brandt, D. (2011). Wikipedia Watch. Retrieved February 6, 2011 from http://www.wikipedia-watch.org

- Spoerri, A. (2007). What is Popular on Wikipedia and Why? *First Monday, 12*(4). Retrieved February 6, 2011 from http://firstmonday.org/htbin/cgiwrap/bin/ojs/index.php/fm/article/view/1765/1645

- *The Economist.* (2006, April 22). The Wiki Principle. Retrieved from http://www.economist.com/node/6794228?story_id=6794228

- Seigenthaler, J. (2005, November 29). A false Wikipedia 'biography'. *USA Today*. Retrieved from http://www.usatoday.com/news/opinion/editorials/2005-11-29-wikipedia-edit_x.htm

- Journalism.org. (2005, October 1). Seigenthaler and Wikipedia: A Case Study on the Veracity of the "Wiki" concept [Web log comment]. Message posted to http://www.journalism.org/node/1672

- Matei, S. A. (2008). How to use wikipedia. Retrieved February 6, 2001 from http://wikiway.net/index.php5?title=How_to_use_wikipedia

OPTIONAL:
- Goetz, T. (2003). Open Source Everywhere. *Wired, 11*(11). Retrieved from http://www.wired.com/wired/archive/11.11/opensource.html

- Pink, D. H. (2005). The Book Stops Here. *Wired, 13*(3). Retrieved from http://www.wired.com/wired/archive/13.03/wiki.html

- timothy. (2005, April 18). The Early History of Nupedia and Wikipedia: A Memoir [Web log comment]. Message posted to http://features.slashdot.org/story/05/04/18/164213/The-Early-History-of-Nupedia-and-Wikipedia-A-Memoir

The social-psychological foundations of virtual communities and online behavior (part I)
- **What are the main socio-psychological processes we should take into account before engaging in the design process?**
- **What are the main dimensions of any online community, according to Baym?**
- **What is the main goal of design: empowering individuals or empowering communities?**

1. Walther, J. B., & Parks, M. R. (2002). Cues filtered out, cues filtered in: Computer-mediated communication and relationships. In M. L. Knapp & J. A. Daly (Eds.), *Handbook of interpersonal communication* (3rd ed., pp. 529-563). Thousand Oaks, CA: Sage.

 2. Kiesler, S., Siegel, J., & McGuire, T. W. (1984). Social psychological aspects of computer-mediated communication. *American Psychologist, 39*(10), 1123-1134.

3. Baym, N. (1998). The emergence of on-line community. In S. Jones (Ed.), *Cybersociety 2.0* (pp. 35-68). Thousand Oaks, CA: Sage.

The social-psychological foundations of online communities (part II)
*   **Summarize the main findings of the literature listed below.**
*   **What is its main conclusion?**
*   **What tools can we use for building strong online communities?**

1. Ling, K., Beenen, G., Ludford, P., Wang, X., Chang, K., Li, X., . . . Kraut, R. (2005). Using Social Psychology to Motivate Contributions to Online Communities. *Journal of Computer-Mediated Communication, 10*(4), article 10.

2. Ridings, C. & Gefen, D. (2004). Virtual Community Attraction: Why People Hang Out Online. *Journal of Computer-Mediated Communication, 10*(1), article 4.

3. Lampe, C., & Resnick, P. (2004). Slash(dot) and burn: distributed moderation in a large online conversation space. In *Proceedings of the ACM Computer Human Interaction Conference 2004* (pp. 543-550). New York, NY: ACM.

4. Cosley, D., Frankowski, D., Kiesler, S., Terveen, L., & Riedl, J. (2005, April). *How oversight improves member-maintained communities.* Paper presented at the Conference on Human Factors in Computing Systems, Portland, OR.

5. Wilson, C. (2008, February 22). The Wisdom of the Chaperones. *Slate.* Retrieved from http://www.slate.com/id/2184487

6. Ludford, P. J., Cosley, D., Frankowski, D., & Terveen, L. (2004). Think different: increasing online community participation using uniqueness and group dissimilarity. In *CHI '04: Proceedings of the SIGCHI Conference on Human Factors in Computing Systems* (pp. 631-638). New York, NY: ACM.

Author Biographies

Sorin Adam Matei was educated at Bucharest University (B.A. in History and Philosophy), Tufts University (Fletcher School of Law and Diplomacy, M.A. in International Relations), and the University of Southern California (Annenberg School for Communication, Ph.D. in Communication). He is currently an Associate Professor of Communication at Purdue University in West Lafayette, Indiana, and Chief Ideamonger at Ideagora (http://ideagora.us), a new media company he founded in 2008. His greatest passion is to create new ways of connecting real and virtual spaces. He has published papers and developed software that aim to make this into a reality. Among the tools he has created are:

- Visible Effort: http://veffort.us
- Thought Ark: http://thoughtark.com
- Alterpode: http://alterpode.net
- Visible Past: http://visiblepast.net
- Ubimark: http://ubimark.com/in

His research has been funded by Motorola, Kettering Foundation, the University of Kentucky, and Purdue University and he has been recognized by various professional organizations with paper and research awards. Dr. Matei teaches the Online Interaction doctoral seminar at Purdue University, Web 2.0 production, and research methods classes. His papers can be found on his Web site http://matei.org/ithink and his classes on his teaching wikis, Wikiway (http://wikiway.net) and Visible Effort (http://veffort.us).

Dr. Matei is a former BBC World Service journalist and is still actively involved with journalistic projects. His columns, photographs, and essays have been published in Esquire Magazine, Foreign Policy and the top national  Romanian language newspapers. He is also the author of the Romanian language books *The Mind Boyars* (http://matei.org/boyars) and *Idols of the Forum* (http://idolii.com), and the publisher of Pagini.com (http://pagini.com).

Brian C. Britt is a Ph.D. student in communication at Purdue University. His research primarily focuses on new media and the ways in which it influences individuals' behavior within formal and informal organizations. In his current research, Britt considers systems of online and offline collaboration and the strategic maneuvering of individual actors within collaboration networks. He aims to enhance the understanding of communication practices within modern organizations in order to improve their formation and processes.

Susan Huelsing Sarapin is a doctoral candidate in the Department of Communication at Purdue University specializing in the confluence of media, technology, and society. Drawing from her years of experience in the fields of medical illustration, advertising, corporate identity design, copywriting, and Web site design, Sarapin currently focuses on media effects. Her major interest area is the intersection of crime-oriented, television fiction (COTV) and the criminal justice system. As such, her major research continues to home in on the effects of exposure to COTV programming on

 juror behavior in regard to self-efficacy in the evaluation of scientific forensic evidence, deliberation discourse, and verdict tendencies. Other interests of hers include political communication and the use of religious themes and images in the advertising of non-religious products.

Pamela Morris is currently a Ph.D. student in Communication at Purdue University. Her interests are collaborative computing and technology adoption in organizations. As a graduate student she works as a research assistant with both the Regenstrief Institute for Healthcare Engineering and the Department of Organizational Leadership and Supervision's Hub Collaboration Research Team. Morris studied computer science and worked at IBM for 12 years before returning to school at Purdue. She aspires to work in corporate research when she completes her degree.

Brenda Berkelaar (M.A., Seton Hall, Ph.D. Purdue University) is an Assistant Professor at University of Texas, Austin. Her research examines the intersections between technology, organizations, careers, learning, and leadership. Berkelaar's dissertation examined *cyber-vetting*, the use of "personal" information to evaluate or profile prospective job candidates. Her current collaborations include studies on online information provision and academic leadership, as well as a funded multi-national project examining children's career perceptions. Berkelaar had authored and co-authored various publications including a recent *Communication Yearbook* chapter, edited book chapters, and journal publications. Prior to enrolling at Purdue,

Berkelaar worked in independent consulting and academic technology.

Robert N. Yale earned an M.A. in speech communication from Miami University (Ohio) and is currently a  doctoral candidate and graduate lecturer in the Department of Communication at Purdue University. His primary area of research interest is persuasion and single-event decision making in high-stakes situations, including legal, health, and business contexts. His dissertation research involves developing a measure of narrative believability – the amalgam of qualities that determine acceptance or rejection of a given narrative in terms of its persuasive impact. Rob's research has been presented at the annual meetings of the Central States Communication Association, the National Communication Association, and the International Communication Association, and has been published in the *Journal of Health Communication*, *Journal of Psychosocial Oncology*, and the *International Journal of Pharmaceutical Compounding*, among other outlets.

Christina Kalinowski is a recent graduate of Purdue University, having earned her Master's Degree in Sociology in the spring of 2009. While her passion for sociology remains strong, communication studies have recently piqued her interest. Her thesis pays tribute to this, serving as an amalgamation of these two disciplines. Entitled "Goffman Meets Online Dating: Exploring the 'Virtually' Socially Produced Self," her thesis focuses on the ways in which members of an online dating Web site present themselves to others and explores the ways in which these presentations of self are influenced over time.

 **W. Scott Sanders** received his M.A. in communication from Purdue University and is currently pursuing a Ph.D. at the USC Annenberg School of Communication. His research interests focus on the communicative and psychological aspects of online communities and mobile telephony. Specifically, he is interested in how people develop trust, evaluate and manage information, and select between mediated channels in relationships that span a variety of media. Sanders is active in several research projects conducted by the Annenberg Program on Online Community and is currently a member of the LIFE Community research team exploring social support and information dissemination among pediatric cancer survivors using mobile social networking.